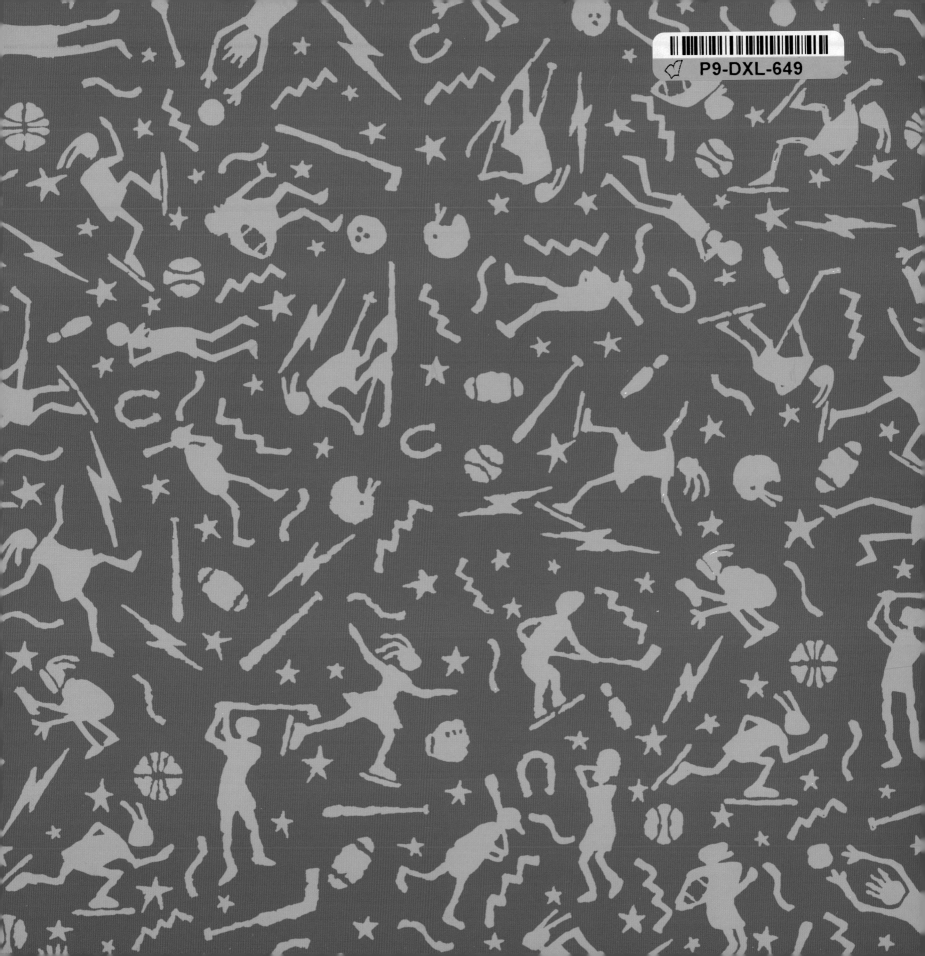

LOCKER ROOM MOJO

TRUE TALES OF SUPERSTITIONS IN SPORTS

Nick Newton & Bill Minutaglio

Designed & Illustrated By Nick Newton

ISBN: 0-9670466-4-5

Library of Congress Catalog Card Number: 99-61075

Printed in Singapore by Kay Lau & Associates
First Edition

Typography from www.t26font.com

Middlefork Press
1009 Madrone Road Austin, Texas 78746
mfpress@aol.com

To those
who *still believe*
in the magic.

ACKNOWLEDGEMENTS

Very special thanks to: John Halligan of the National Hockey League, John McClain of the Houston Chronicle, Joe Hoppel and Mike Nahrstedt at The Sporting News, Mike Zagaris, Don Hunter, Ron Kuntz, H. Lane Stewart, Alan Dockery and Thomas Burrell for their generous and creative contributions to this book.

Sincere Appreciation to: Tim Wiles, Tim Bottorff, Bill Burdick and Darcy Harrington at The National Baseball Hall of fame / Saleem Choudhry at The Pro football Hall of fame / Phil Pritchard at The Hockey Hall of fame / Donald Davison at The Indianapolis Motor Speedway Hall of fame / Don Namath and Jim freeman at The International Motor Sports Hall of fame / Bob Curran, Jr. and Tom Merritt at The Thoroughbred Racing Commission / R.C. Owens and Kirk Reynolds at The San fransisco 49ers / George Goad at formula One Spectators Association / Cindy Hoppner and Andrew Enzisco at The Make-A-Wish foundation / Mike Altieri at The Los Angeles Kings / Brad Joyal at The Ottawa Senators / Bernie Stowe at the Cincinnatti Reds / Kathy Lauterbach at Newman-Haas Racing / Mike Norris and Andrea fisher at Centre College / Cathy Schneck at Keeneland Library / Mike Mooney at Hollywood Park / Josephine Impastato and Rich Pilling at Major League Baseball / Kris Hook at Bettman Archives / Lee Allen at New York folklore Quarterly / Doug Miller at the New York Jets / Tessa Atkins at the Tennessee Oilers / Glen Serra at the Atlanta Braves / Deb Williams at Winston Cup Scene / John Heisler at Notre Dame University / Ed Carpenter and Mike Eruzione at Boston University / Tracey at MLB Alumni Association / Jack Reynolds / Mark fidrych / Russ francis / Eric Wunderlich at U.S. Swimming / Dan Colchico / Eddie frierson / Jim and Cindy Carroccio and "Rojo" from the Austin Zoo / John "Big Dawg" Thompson / George Allison / Sam Siaris / Des Byrne / Pat Novack / Charles Henderson / John Collantine / Dennis and Mary Broadway / Carsten Zatchler / Nick geddes / Alex O'Reilly / Rob Titherly at The Brooklands Society / Andrew at PhotoSport / Amy Drackert / Kathleen Devigne / Mike Mullis / Bill Cannon / Nadia Guerriero / Marc and Carol McClure / Jo and Peter Stougaard / Amy Rojas / Dan Arriola / Skip Pratt / Aitken fruean / Melissa Wagamon / Daniel Mejia-Onat / Andrew gaze / Bob Willer / Mark Rucker at Transcendental Graphics / Peter Dransfield / Rey Mena / Tom Bukur / Greg Harrison / Pete King / Kay Lau for her support and guidance / Gina Petrella / Anne O'Conor Newton / Dennis Newton / Teddy Seraphine / Erik Torgerson / Carlos Segura and T26 / and to Jill Newton for her love, patience, support, and dining room table.

CONTENTS

The '73 Mets had a slogan.

Ya Gotta Believe.

And that's what Mojo is all about. Either you believe or you don't believe. It's about the art of the possible when you're playing a game. It's about faith so strong that you can move mountains ~ or at least move runners from first to third. It's about athletic magic ~ the same kind of magic in "The Field of Dreams" and "Hoosiers" and "The Natural." It's about looking for an edge, a higher authority, a bit of luck, a tender mercy from on high. It's about trying anything that gets you bragging rights at the 19th Hole, that massive rainbow trout, that sub-4-minute mile, that perfect slapshot and that perfect game.

But there's something else.

Mojo is all about the innocence of sports before everything got all murky, monied and awkward, before sports got endlessly analyzed ~ as if every minute of every game, every match, every race got poked and prodded until all the mystery seeped out the holes.

Mojo is by its very existence a big, fine, fat mystery. It can't be analyzed. It's not in its nature.

How do you measure magic? How do you explain how the 70-1 horse thunders home first? How do you explain the hole-in-one?

It's the thing that links the little boy in Babe Ruth with the little girl in Picabo Street. It's the thing that you might very well find if you dig and scratch far enough back in your mind ~ as if you were combing through your closet for that battered baseball mitt or your rusty pair of skates. Something that you might remember feeling the first time you saw Pete Maravich yank that invisible string on a basketball. Something you might have felt in your soul when you first heard Lou Gehrig's mournful, triumphant, goodbye speech ~ a dying man saying that he was the luckiest person on the face of the earth because he had been allowed to play a kid's game. It could even be something you might have seen in Michael Jordan's face ~ in the way his tongue wags when he is so deliriously, completely absorbed in the utter wonder of what he does better than anyone else.

Call it purity, call it magic, call it Mojo.

Ya Gotta Believe.

Bad Intentions...

THE CURSE

OF THE

BAMBINO

It began on January 5th, 1920 when Boston Red Sox™ owner Harry Frazee stunned the Red Sox faithful by announcing the sale of their star, George Herman "Babe" Ruth to the New York Yankees™ for $125,000 cash and a $300,000 loan for a mortgage on Fenway Park. Frazee, a theatrical producer who genuinely loved baseball, but loved Broadway more, saw his team as an alternative source of financing for his theatrical operations.

Shortly after purchasing the club in 1917, Frazee needed to raise cash for several Broadway ventures so he began selling off the team's stars, one by one to Colonel Jacob Rupert owner of the New York Yankees. During the Red Sox's greatest years, Ruth was their greatest player, winning 89 games as a pitcher in six years. Pitching in two World Series™, he threw a series record

Babe as a rookie with the Red Sox in 1915.

The vilified Red Sox owner Harry Frazee.

29 2/3 scoreless innings, a record that stood for 43 years.

In 1919 the Babe was moved to the outfield so that he could hit more often. That year he hit 29 home runs, the most ever hit in a single season by any player. In 1920, Ruth hit 54 home runs for New York, more than all but one team managed to hit all that year.

The Yankees have won 35 pennants, and 24 World Series titles. The Red Sox never recovered. They had won five of the first fifteen World Series. They would not play in another one for more than a quarter century. Since Ruth left, the Red Sox have won four pennants and no World Series™, losing Game 7 in 1946 and 1967 to St. Louis, in 1975 to Cincinnati and in 1986 to the Mets™. The legacy continues.

CAPTAIN'S CURSE

Leadership has its pitfalls – unless, for some reason, there is a ton of money thrown in to ease the headaches of being on top. Consider the Captain's Curse, a wicked case of Reverse Mojo that hit some hockey players just when they thought their fortunes were on the rise: Through the 1990s, a series of four Montreal Canadiens™™ team captains wound up being unceremoniously traded – including Chris Chelios and Guy Carbonneau. The old Ottawa Senators™™ invented the name for it – the Captain's Curse – after they went through five captains in two years.

If Looks Could Kill...

THE ITALIANS CALL IT 'MALOCCHIO', IN ENGLISH IT IS SIMPLY KNOWN AS THE 'EVIL EYE'. WHATEVER YOU CALL IT, AS FAR AS BAD MOJO GOES...IT'S THE WORST.

THE EFFECTS OF EVEN A GLANCE FROM THE 'EVIL EYE' ARE SAID TO BRING MAJOR MISFORTUNE TO ITS TARGET.

ACCORDING TO 'THE ENCYCLOPEDIA OF SIGNS, OMENS AND SUPERSTITIONS', THE BELIEF WAS INSPIRED BY THE BIBLICAL PHRASE "EAT THOU NOT THE BREAD OF HIM THAT HATH THE EVIL EYE" (PROVERBS 23:6).

IN MEDIEVAL TIMES, IF SOMEONE WERE BELIEVED TO HAVE USED THE EVIL EYE TO INFLICT HARM ON ANOTHER PERSON, THEY WERE TRIED FOR WITCHCRAFT, AND MORE OFTEN THAN NOT, BURNED AT THE STAKE.

DURING HIS PLAYING DAYS, HOCKEY HALL OF FAMER PHIL ESPOSITO WAS CONSIDERED ONE OF THE MORE MOJO-CONSCIOUS PLAYERS IN THE NHL. ESPO WOULD RECEIVE ALL SORTS OF GOOD-LUCK CHARMS FROM FANS, WHICH HE WOULD POST AROUND HIS LOCKER, HOPING TO FIND THE RIGHT ONE. HIS PRE-GAME ROUTINE WOULD INCLUDE: FOLLOWING THE SAME PATTERN OF DRESSING (INCLUDING AN OLD BLACK T-SHIRT WHICH HAD TO BE WORN INSIDE-OUT), TAKING HIS CHEWING GUM FROM A NEW PACK AND HIS TAPE FROM A FRESH ROLL. AND IF ESPO SAW TWO STICKS CROSSED IN THE DRESSING ROOM, HE WOULD GO BERSERK.

PHIL'S MOST POTENT SUPERSTITION, HOWEVER, WAS HIS STRONG BELIEF IN 'MALOCCHIO'. HE WAS SURE THAT IF SOMEONE CROSSED THROUGH HIS BEAM OF ILL-INTENT, THEY WOULD BE HEXED WITH BAD MOJO IN THE EXTREME.

HIS PLAYING DAYS OVER, ESPO NOW WORKS AT THE EXECUTIVE LEVEL IN HOCKEY WHERE HE CAN HURL HIS GLANCE FROM A DESK INSTEAD OF A PENALTY BOX. AND WHILE THINGS CAN GET PRETTY HOT IN THE FRONT OFFICE, PHIL IS NO DOUBT GLAD THE WITCH TRIALS ARE OVER. THAT KIND OF HEAT WOULD BE TOUGH TO TAKE.

BILLY GOAT'S CURSE

On October 6, 1945 Chicago tavern owner, William "Billy Goat" Sianis, tried to take his pet goat, Sonovia, to Wrigley Field to catch the fourth game of the 1945 World Series™ against Detroit. Of course, the Cubs refused to let the goat through the turnstiles.

Sianis was furious. It wasn't the seven dollars and twenty cents apiece Sianis coughed up for the tickets, it was the principle. Billy Goat

"Billy Goat" and Sonovia wait for P. K. Wrigley.

in the park.

Sianis was more than mad. He was vexed to the point of laying a hex. He cursed the team, assuring Wrigley that they would not only lose this series, but they would never again reach the fall classic.

On October 10, Detroit won game seven and the series. That very afternoon Billy Goat sent a telegram to P. K. Wrigley that read: "Who smells now?"

had attended games at Wrigley with his beloved Sonovia that very season. He demanded to speak to Cubs' owner and chewing-gum king Phillip K. Wrigley. When Wrigley arrived on the scene, he supported the decision to keep Sianis' bearded friend from attending the game. When Sianis persisted for an explanation, Wrigley simply stated that his goat smelled and would not be allowed

Sonovia's unused ticket.

The curse prevailed.

Since that day, the Cubbies have yet to win another pennant. In 1969, a year before he passed away, Billy Goat temporarily removed the hex when the Cubs took a huge lead in their division going into August. It looked as though The Curse was lifted at long last, but the Cubs folded to the "Miracle Mets" at the wire.

Sam Sianis, Billy Goat's nephew and heir to the tavern, renewed the hex in 1973 when he tried, unsuccessfully, to bring his goat 'Socrates' to Wrigley for a game. At the time, the Cubs had a seven game lead in first place, but dropped it in just two weeks.

Cub management has owned up to the dark mojo engendered by the goat, allowing a beer company to use the Cubs logo in ads that featured a talking, wiseguy goat promising to lift The Curse if he is offered a big fat brewski.

Sam may be feeling a little guilty about The Curse. He showed up on The Tonight Show, promising Jay Leno that The Curse could be lifted, while he paraded his goat onto the stage Sam formally declared the hex removed.

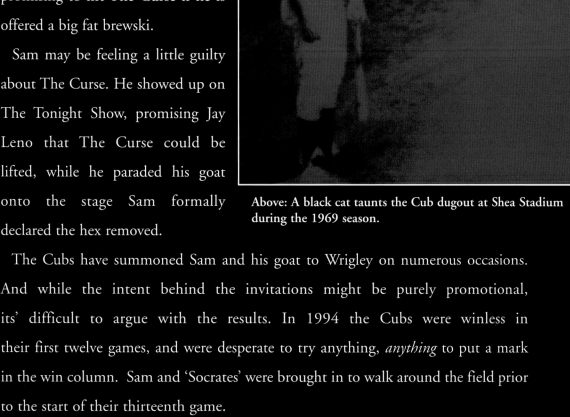

Above: A black cat taunts the Cub dugout at Shea Stadium during the 1969 season.

Sam Sianis leads 'Socrates' on a hex-lifting stroll at Wrigley Field.

The Cubs have summoned Sam and his goat to Wrigley on numerous occasions. And while the intent behind the invitations might be purely promotional, its' difficult to argue with the results. In 1994 the Cubs were winless in their first twelve games, and were desperate to try anything, *anything* to put a mark in the win column. Sam and 'Socrates' were brought in to walk around the field prior to the start of their thirteenth game.

The Cubbies notched their first win of the season that day.

The Curse Of The Ages

Red Dutton (back row, fifth from left) as a player with the New York Americans squad of 1933-34.

One of the greatest, lingering curses in professional sports saddled the hapless New York Rangers™ for over a half-century.

In 1942, Mervyn "Red" Dutton, then manager of the New York Americans™ hockey team, decided that he would levy a heavy fine against the New York Rangers - he boldly asserted that the New York Rangers "will never win another Cup in my lifetime."

The cause for his bitter declaration was his belief that the Rangers were responsible for doing everything in their power to oust his team from Madison Square Garden (which owned the Rangers), ultimately causing their demise.

Red's curse held.

He passed away in 1987 and the Rangers' still hadn't brought home another championship. New York fans grew accustomed to watching some pretty good Ranger teams somehow crumble in the playoffs and perpetually fall short of the Stanley Cup™. History-minded fans from other teams knew that the best way to unnerve the Rangers was to shout "1940" over and over again - a subtle reminder to say the least.

The curse seemed impenetrable and there is no exact word on whether the Rangers resorted to some supreme Mojo authority to have it lifted - but they finally won another championship in 1994.

In a last attempt to generate enough public interest to save his team, Red changed the name of the club to the Brooklyn Americans.
It was too little, too late.

The Season of the Witch

Opening day in baseball is supposed to be a joyous occasion. America's favorite pastime returneth. For those whose teams were a disappointment last season, it's a fresh start, everybody is undefeated. And for the rest of the nation, sports fans or not, it is the annual proclamation that winter is over and spring has returned once again.

Opening day of 1998 should have been doubly joyous for the Arizona Diamondbacks™. They were Major League Baseball's™ newest expansion team, and they had a fancy new $354 million dollar home, complete with a high-tech, retractable-roof, paid for in part with taxpayer's dollars.

But not everybody loves baseball. And the idea of having to kick in out-of-pocket to build baseball a home in their own backyard made one group of folks pretty upset.

The Libertarians were in that group.

They were upset over the idea that the city would increase the sales tax a quarter-cent in order to raise the requisite $238 million without voter consent. They were upset that all their legal challenges, including a referendum drive, were unsuccessful. And they had decided that the only option left was to put a hex on the Arizona Diamondbacks and their fans as a protest...on opening day.

On March 31, 1998, while the Diamondbacks played the first game in franchise history against the Colorado Rockies™, the Libertarians assembled outside Bank One Ballpark in Phoenix. They had invited three witches and a medicine man to the site in order to cast spells on the place. One witch apparently couldn't make it, but was able to fling her mojo 'telephonically' through a Libertarian party member's cell phone.

The Diamondbacks lost their first 5 games. And by mid-April, they had won only 2 of their first 15 games. At the end of the season it appeared that the witches had done the job. The Arizona team finished last in the Western Division with a miserable record of 65 wins and 97 losses.

The only consolation, if any, was the knowledge that two teams had finished with worse records.

For the Diamondbacks, 1998 was truly the 'season of the witch'.

THE CURSE OF THE RAINBOW JERSEY

The Czech belief regarding rainbows is that if you point at one...you will cause thunder and your finger will fall from your hand. While you might think that a bit strange, consider their neighbor to the south. In Yugoslavia, if someone crosses through the end of the rainbow, they will quite simply change sex. The most common belief is that where a rainbow touches the ground, a pot of gold may be found.

This is probably more in line with the thinking that goes on in the minds of the world's most elite group of cyclists as they race to win the World Cycling Championship and the coveted rainbow jersey awarded to its winner every year.

But capturing the rainbow jersey may be more of a curse than a blessing. Consider some of the most recent past recipients:

- *Irishman Stephen Roche won the title in 1987 after winning the Tour de France in the same season. He then underwent knee surgery (for the third time), and his career was never the same.*
- *In 1955, Stan Ockers of Belgium won it, and then died in a racing accident 14 months later.*
- *American legend Greg LeMond won it in 1989 and seemingly avoided the jinx by winning another Tour de France victory in 1990. But he retired four years later after struggling with a rare disease called Muscular Myopathy.*
- *Rudy Dhaenens won it in 1990 only to retire months later after being diagnosed with a heart condition.*
- *American Lance Armstrong became the youngest winner in over 20 years when he won in 1993 and three years later was diagnosed with advanced testicular cancer.*
- *Scotsman Graeme Obree, known for his distinctive ski-tuck racing position, won it in 1995 only to have a virus dash his chance of Olympic glory in Atlanta in 1996.*

The list of hapless victors is long, as is the list of explanations for the possible curse. Coincidences may account for some. There is even a theory that the mystique surrounding the jersey is so public and openly discussed amongst cyclists that they almost expect the misfortune to follow, and when it comes along, they are not surprised. A self-fulfilling prophecy.

THE CURSE OF
Rocky Colavito

Talk about haunted. Talk about what goes around comes around. Talk about The Curse of Rocky Colavito.

The pride and joy of the Cleveland Indians was one of the game's premier sluggers in the late 1950s. And he was, by most estimations, the guy least likely to be traded - Colavito was happy in Cleveland and the fans were happy to have him. The day before the opening game of the 1960 season, Colavito was abruptly dispatched to Detroit for Harvey Kuenn. It was a blockbuster trade of hard-hitting stars (Kuenn had led the American League in hitting the year before; Colavito had belted 42 homers and bagged 111 RBIs). But it quickly became known in the bars, bleachers and backrooms of Cleveland as The Curse of Rocky Colavito:

Kuenn suffered some injuries during the 1960 season and attendance dropped by almost a half-million fans.

Worse, from 1960 to 1993, the Indians finished no higher than third.

In the Beginning...

EARLY RODEO?

THIS FRESCO FROM THE ANCIENT PALACE OF KNOSSOS DEPICTS THREE ATHLETES, OR ONE ATHLETE IN THREE DIFFERENT POSITIONS.

IN THE SECOND OR THIRD MILLENIUM BEFORE THE TIME OF CHRIST, THE MINOANS, OF THE ISLE OF CRETE, PERFORMED AN ATHLETIC RITUAL THEY CALLED 'BULL-LEAPING'. BY TODAY'S STANDARDS THE ACT WOULD BE CONSIDERED PART GYMNASTICS, PART RODEO, AND SO TOTALLY INSANE IT WOULD SURELY GRAB CENTER STAGE AT THE 'X' GAMES.

THE 'BULL-LEAP' BEGINS WHEN A JUMPER SEIZES THE BULL'S HORNS CAUSING THE ANIMAL TO VIOLENTLY THROW BACK HIS HEAD, PROPELLING THE ATHLETE UP AND OVER THE BULL'S BACK.

BECAUSE THE BULL WAS THE SYMBOLIC ANIMAL OF MINOAN CULTURE, AND REPRESENTED AMONG MANY THINGS, THE EMBODIMENT OF MALE POTENCY, IT IS BELIEVED THAT 'BULL-LEAPING' WAS MOST LIKELY A FERTILITY RITE.

WHILE THIS PARTICULAR VERSION OF THE RITUAL VANISHED WITH THE MINOAN CIVILIZATION, A FORM OF 'BULL-LEAPING' IS WIDELY PRACTICED TODAY IN OUR NATION'S CAPITAL.

RISKY BUSINESS

IN MOST SPORTS THE RISK OF INJURY, OR EVEN DEATH,
IS INTRINSIC TO THE GAME.
ATHLETES ACCEPT AND UNDERSTAND THIS.
BUT THE RISK IS NOT THEIRS ALONE.
ASK THE FAN WHO TOOK THE LINE DRIVE
FOUL BALL IN THE SIDE OF THE HEAD.
ASK THE FAMILY OF FOUR THAT GOT
PLOWED FROM THEIR SEATS BY THE
SIX-FOOT-TEN FORWARD WHO FAILED
TO KEEP THE BALL INBOUNDS.
THE SPECTATOR IS OFTEN MORE THAN JUST
WITNESS TO THE ACTION.
BUT WE ACCEPT THE RISKS.
WE ACCEPT THEM FROM
THE MOMENT THE
USHER TEARS
THE TICKET IN
HALF AND HANDS
IT BACK. JUST LOOK AT THE BACK
OF YOUR TICKET THE NEXT TIME YOU
GO TO A BALL GAME. READ THE FINE
PRINT...WE'RE ON OUR OWN.
THAT POINT WAS NEVER MADE MORE CLEAR
THAN IT WAS BACK IN 7TH CENTURY BC. BECAUSE THE ATHLETES
COMPETED NAKED, WOMEN WERE FORBIDDEN TO ATTEND THE OLYMPIC
GAMES. IT WAS BAD MOJO, AND ANY WOMAN CAUGHT VIEWING THE COMPETITION WOULD BE THROWN TO HER DEATH FROM
A NEARBY CLIFF. IT WAS A HIGHLY PUBLICIZED FACT. AND IT WAS RESPECTED.
THE ONLY RECORDED INSTANCE OF A VIOLATION OF THAT LAW WAS
BY A WOMAN NAMED KALLIPATEIRA. KALLIPATEIRA'S FATHER THREE BROTHERS, NEPHEW AND SON WERE ALL OLYMPIC
VICTORS. WHEN HER HUSBAND DIED, SHE TRAINED HER SON BY HERSELF. WHEN SHE BROUGHT HIM TO OLYMPIA TO COMPETE SHE
DISGUISED HERSELF AS A MALE TRAINER AND ENTERED THE STADIUM WITH HIM. HER SON WAS VICTORIOUS AND
WHEN SHE LEAPT OVER THE BARRIER TO CONGRATULATE HIM, HER CLOTHES CAME OFF, REVEALING TO EVERYONE THAT SHE
WAS A WOMAN. IT WAS DECIDED THAT BECAUSE HER FAMILY HAD SUCH A CELEBRATED HISTORY AT THE GAMES...IN ORDER TO
HONOUR THEM, SHE WOULD NOT BE PUNISHED, AFTER THIS INCIDENT HOWEVER, IT WAS DECIDED THAT TRAINERS WOULD
ALSO BE REQUIRED TO BE NAKED AT THE OLYMPIC GAMES, MAKING IT IMPOSSIBLE FOR WOMEN TO ENTER IN DISGUISE.

BAGGATAWAY...

...Istaboli, Tolik...different tribes called it by different names, but they all meant the same thing...Little Brother of War.

We know it as Lacrosse. The game played today, however, bears little resemblance to this Mojo-Monster of a war game that, only two hundred years ago, had tribes from Canada all the way to the south tip of Florida settling major differences through this often very bloody and always spiritual game.

When news of a game got out thousands could be expected to show up, loaded down with worldly posessions ready to wager on the game's outcome. The game itself would be played on a field about 220 feet long, with 20-foot high goalposts erected at either end. In preparation, members of each team, sometimes numbering as many as 100 per side, would paint their bodies and drink sacred medicine. Meanwhile, tribal medicine men would do battle with each other, hurling their best Mojo incantations and believing their magic would strengthen their own team, while weakening the other. Players armed simply with a webbed stick (or sticks), would approach each other from opposite sides of the field and play would ensue when a tribal elder threw the skin-covered ball into play.

24

Heads Up... ...or... Heads Off!

Good pre-game locker room advice if you're an Aztec ballplayer around 1000 A.D. In what may be an early ancestor to what we know as basketball, players who failed to win had a lot more at stake than riding the pine or being shipped off to some desolate triple-A outpost. Losing a game would often mean losing your head. The earliest version of the game can be traced all the way back to the 10th century B.C. Olmecs who played it as a fertility rite at religious festivals. The Aztec version was played on courts as long as 300 feet with walls 12 feet high. There were temples at both ends and wooden or stone rings set into the middle of the walls on both sides. After a rubber ball, weighing several pounds,

was tossed into play, players would pass it to their teammates using their hips, elbows, legs and heads (using hands or feet was prohibited). The object of the game was to hit the ball up and through the ring to score and win (the first team to score won the contest). The movement of the ball and the way in which victory was achieved were believed to suggest various omens, revealing the profound religious importance the game held on its society. The winning team had the right to grab jewelry and clothing from any spectators who could'nt get away fast enough, while the losers paid the ultimate price...they were beheaded as a sacrifice to the gods.

At first glance, a Sumo match appears to be about two severely overweight guys, naked, save for a very colorful, pamper-like device around their valuables, lunging and crashing into one another. Each trying to push the other out of a big, round sandbox.

Well...ok, that's pretty accurate. But there is much, *much* more to this 2000 year old sport that is considered Japan's national pastime.

Also thought to be the first martial art, Sumo wrestling's origins are deeply rooted in Japan's oldest religion, *Shinto,* which account for the heavily ritualistic ceremony that pervades all aspects of a Sumo bout.

When the wrestlers, or *'Rikishi'*, first enter the ring they clap their hands loudly to attract the Gods' attention, and proclaim their own purity of heart and purpose. They slowly raise their right legs, as high as possible, and bring them crashing down with tremendous force. They then perform the same earth-shaking stomp with the left legs. This act is called the *'shiko'*, and is meant to drive evil spirits from the ring.

Salt is then thrown by the Rikishi in order to purify the ring after the last bout's loss. The two warriors now face each other in the middle of the ring, each trying to intimidate the other with stares. Finally, with a word from the referee, they squat, lean forward, touch hands on the ground and then crash into each other at full force. The fight itself is brief, but fierce. The first wrestler to set a foot or any other part of his body outside the ring, or touch the ground inside the ring with anything but the sole of his foot, loses.

Ranking is based on a pyramid system. from novice (Jonokuchi), at the bottom, to Grand Champions (Yokozunas), at the top. Ironically, the current Yokozuna is an American from Hawaii by the name of Akebono.

The Sumo *elite* enjoy celebrity status on a par with movie stars and rock musicians in Japan. Some have their own fan clubs, web sites, even trading cards.

Hey Yoshi...trade you two Mark McGwires for an Akebono!

Bowling for Salvation

The first record of bowling as game or sport was Kegelspiel (pin-game), developed in Germany sometime in the Middle Ages. The pins themselves, when not being used in a game, were used as excercisers for arms and carried around for self defense. People often carried them to church, which is probably where the clergy, acknowledging its extreme popularity among the masses and recognizing the potential of Kegelspiel as a tool, sanctioned the game. The church declared the pins to be symbols of paganism, very bad mojo, and to bowl them down was a metaphorical blow for good over evil.

While the object of Kegelspiel was similar to modern bowling, any number of pins might be used. That is until the 16th century when Martin Luther, the reformer, first declared the ideal number of pins to be nine. Thus the game was known as Nine-pin bowling until the 1840's when the tenth pin was added.

Aside from the really cool shirts and the smelly shoes they make us rent, little about bowling has changed.

Animal Attraction...

Saddled By Bad Luck

Phar Lap, the immortal Australian thoroughbred, is connected to one of the more chilling Mojo Moments in sports history. After the horse died in California (in what newspapers described as "mysterious" circumstances), Phar Lap's Australian jockey decided that the horse's saddle was just too lucky to be disposed of.

He ceremoniously presented it to a renowned rider named George "The Iceman" Woolf. The new owner was very pleased with the over-sized saddle, made from a special combination of kangaroo hide and snakeskin. In time, Woolf began using the saddle as often as he could. It became, of course, his personal Track Mojo. He even used the saddle on one of the greatest thoroughbreds ever - Seabiscuit - during some famous duels with War Admiral.

But, on Jan. 3, 1946, Woolf was thrown from a horse named Please Me at the Santa Anita track. Woolf eventually died from his injuries.

When friends went through his personal belongings, they found his Mojo Saddle inside his trunk. For some reason on that day at Santa Anita, Woolf had decided he didn't need it.

No other bird has stirred the collective imagination, nor ignited such heated debate over it's varied reputation, as the peacock.

Considered by some cultures to be a bird of divinity, the peacock is more often blamed as a bird whose presence forebodes evil intent.

In India for instance, the Hindus believe the bird has angel's feathers, a devil's voice, and a thief's walk, with the ability to warn of evil. They revere peacocks as birds of magic, good fortune to have around. On the other hand, in Italy and many other parts of the world, the feather is associated with 'Malocchio', or the 'Evil Eye', and is thought to bring nothing but bad luck.

This was probably the opinion of the jockeys and trainers at Santa Anita Racetrack in Arcadia, California. Before the start of the 1934 season, the track was offered a number of peacocks by the Lucky Baldwin Estate. The management accepted them with the idea that placing them in the infield would add to the track's natural beauty, like the flamingos at Hialeah.

The horsemen went berserk. The surprised management quickly learned of the peacock's reputation as bad mojo, and the birds were promptly evicted.

A BiRd moSt FoUl

Hockey fans love to throw things on the ice - and anyone who has ever watched some old-school, hard-checking, high-sticking amateur hockey has even seen people slip nuts, bolts and batteries over the boards. Sometimes, it simply isn't a pretty picture.

In early October 1995, a winger for the Florida Panthers™ named Scott Mellanby spied the same thing that everyone else in the locker room was hooting and hollering about. A rat had unceremoniously made its way into the Panthers dressing room just as the team was getting ready to hit the ice for the first game of the season at home. While the burly men of hockey yelled and hollered, Mellanby decided to take the rat matters into his own quick, deft hands. He measured the rat and then slap-shot the creature into the great Rat Goal in the Sky.

That night, Mellanby skated marvelously and bagged two goals in a rousing 4-3 win over the Calgary Flames™. Word spread about Mellanby's skills in Rat Removal and suddenly the rat was viewed as the ultimate good luck tool.

The rest of the rat story is history. Florida Panthers' fans quickly adopted one of the more endearing bits of Mojo in all of sports –
the art of winging plastic rats
(and the occasional real one)
onto the ice.

the RAT TRICK

Some of these guys work well as a team. They live on the high plains. They can work at altitudes that most people cannot survive. They are accustomed to performing solitary, single tasks. They actually have the ability to carry heavy loads - maybe up to 100 pounds. Some of them have long necks, big ears and droopy faces.

All of it could describe your average baseball player. And, if someone in the Texas Rangers™ had their way, they might have actually used these llamas as part of the bullpen - or maybe as the occasional designated hitter. The strange but true saga of the amazing Texas Rangers' Llamas is one of the more unsual mojo moments in professional sports.

It seems that Rangers' management - weary of the Texas team never being able to offer any consistent highlights (except, of course, for the amazing Nolan Ryan, Juan Gonzalez and Ivan "Punch" Rodriguez) - once decided to import some Peruvian pack animals from the high plains of the Andes to the high plains of Arlington, Texas.

While the struggling Rangers were playing pepper and taking batting practice, the llamas were paraded onto the field and circled around the bases as a way to bring some form of good luck to the team. A few of the players apparently began eye-balling the llamas in a Reverse Mojo way: there was some quiet speculation about what llama barbecue would taste like.

The South American relative of the camel family has had a winning tradition that traces back to the days of the Incas. The same, unfortunately, cannot be said of the Texas Rangers - despite the llama's best efforts. But, either way, the team definitely wins Mojo Points for the most creative use of the animal that is known as the camel-without-a-hump.

400

IF YOU GOT THE BUNNY HONEY, I GOT THE GUN!

Chalk it all up to some mighty Mojo Hand pressing down out of that sometimes
unbearable Houston humidity. Chalk it up to some pretty unusual habits at the Houston Oilers™.
Finally, chalk it up to some odd developments surrounding the most odd guys on the field
– the punters and kickers who always, always, always seem to tend toward the offbeat.
Former Oilers punter Greg Montgomery liked to keep a giant stuffed rabbit in his locker.
In preparation for an upcoming game, he liked to attach something to the rabbit
– about the next opponent and usually, ahem, something very unflattering.
The Oilers liked his Mojo ritual well enough until he managed to make one of
his own offensive lineman a bit unhappy.
One afternoon, when Montgomery was attending a team meeting, he heard gunshots outside.
Two of the hulking Oilers' linemen had abducted Mr Rabbit, strung him between the goalposts,
found some shotguns and blew the bunny to Mojo Heaven.
The Oilers' famous slogan was "Love You Blue" – maybe it should have been
"Love You Bunny."

The Chicken Men Get Their Hits

When he retires,

Wade Boggs will probably make it into the Hall of Fame as one of the steadiest hitters
in the history of baseball. If he makes it to Cooperstown, they might set up a little chicken coop alongside his
name. Boggs, for years, has drawn strength from The Chicken. Legend has it that he has to have it prepared 50
different ways and that the main reason he won the 1983 batting title was because he had given himself over to the
power of the bird. Boggs of course is multi-denominational when it comes to his mojo. In the batter's box, he would
etch out Hebrew letters for good luck. And, of course, he is a strong believer in 7 and 17: He demanded that the
Boston Red Sox™ pay him $717,000 in 1984 and he takes his wind sprints at 7:17 p.m.

Boggs isn't the only High Priest of the Fowl. Former Pittsburgh Pirates'™ great Vic Davalillo scared his room-mate
on a road trip one time by walking into their hotel room with two very nervous chickens. Davalillo reached inside
the cage and began stroking the birds. His roomie, Jackie Hernandez, was stunned and more than a bit edgy. "It's
good luck to rub a chicken, Jackie," said a deadly serious Davalillo. You'll see. I'll get some hits tomorrow. Want to
pet this one?" Like most bits of mojo, it remains unclear whether Davalillo got his hits the next day.

The "Rain-Meister"

In Folklore, when ducks Flap their wings while swimming, it is a Foretelling of rain. This may explain why Christian Fittipaldi's pit crew has a rubber duck as a mascot. Christian, nephew of the two-time world champion Emerson Fittipaldi, is known on the Indy Car race circuit as the "rain-meister" for his driving prowess on rain-slicked tracks. While most drivers have a tendency to be more cautious and conservative in the rain, Fittipaldi sees it as an opportunity and 'goes for it'.

The Legend Of The Octopus

On April 15, 1952, the Detroit Red Wings™ were in the third game of the second series playoffs against the Montreal Canadiens™ at the Olympic Stadium in Detroit. In the previous series they had eliminated Toronto in four straight games. Two brothers, Pete and Jerry Cusimano, owners of a local fish market and avid Red Wing fans, wanted to do something to help their team. What they came up with was both the slimiest and most original bit of mojo ever put on ice. They decided to use an octopus with its eight tentacles to inspire the Red Wings to win eight games straight, the number needed to win the Stanley Cup™.

Pete Cusimano smuggled the ugly bottom-dweller into the stadium and waited until after the first goal was scored, at which time he lobbed the semi-cooked octopus out onto the ice. The players were perplexed, but they went on to win the Stanley Cup in eight games - the first time ever!

Pete and Jerry's seafood-mojo worked its charm. The octopus has since been considered good luck in hockey, and throwing them onto the ice has become an International tradition.

LIMPING LEPUS

In the giant, endless pantheon of sports figures who allowed themselves to be washed over by a giant wave of Mojo, there have been a handful of superstars who have been completely immersed. They are the ones who were so intertwined with various forms of Mojo that it was almost hard to separate their superstitions from their personalities. Unfortunately for time, poetry and history, it seems that there might be fewer hardcore Mojo-ites these days as opposed to the earlier decades of this century. Today, with so many players using biomechanic engineers, nutritionists and personal statisticians to keep track of every ounce of body fat and every variation in a batting stance, golf swing or free-throw fluidity, it's hard to imagine the kind of mojo that . . . say . . . Joe Medwick was into.

The Hall of Fame baseballer was a high priest in the practice of Mojo. He used to keep a wary eye on anything that could harm him - none of those chalk lines to step on, none of those little bits of paper blowing around the infield, over the mound, near the dugout or the on-deck circle. He also liked to keep a watchful, hopeful, eye on anything that could help him - scoop up those safety pins, scream for great, good joy when you spot a big collection of them spilled across the floor, the street or the locker room floor.

Fans, team-mates, coaches and opposing players would always keep a careful eye on the mercurial Medwick. They respected him and they actually tried to help him on occasion if they saw that there was some kind of mojo he was searching for, hungering for. In 1940, Medwick decided that he had to have a lucky rabbit's foot that a team-mate had been using somewhat successfully to string together some hits.

Medwick decided that the lepus appendage could be part of his own, private arsenal of hoodoo-voodoo techniques. Of course, when he got the rabbit's foot it worked in reverse. The foot had either been drained of power or there was something about Medwick that prevented him from absorbing the foot's power. The disputing debute of the Mojo Bunny Foot led to one of the learned observations in the history of Locker Room Mojo. It will go down as, literally, the famous last words on the entire subject of Mojo in the realm of professional sports: "That rabbit's foot didn't bring me any more luck than it did the rabbit," said the wiser but sadder Medwick.

Its Only Money...

The First Yankee Mascot

It was not big and fluffy. It did not have wild bulging eyes or big floppy feet.

It would not hire itself out for birthday bashes, grand openings or even the occasional

charity fund raiser. It would not even pose for pictures with adoring, eager young fans.

It wasn't indifferent, or callous, or anti-social at all. In fact, it had no attitude

whatsoever. The first Yankee mascot was a common penny. In 1903, when

ground was broken at 168th street and Broadway in New York City,

for what was to be Hilltop Park, the Yankees first American League™ home,

a penny was found. An 1817 copper one-cent piece to be precise.

Joseph W. Gordon, team president and slave to superstition, had the penny mounted,

framed and hung on the wall of his office. Apparently, as a harbinger of good mojo,

the penny worked. The Yankees have brought in quite a few pennies since that day.

A LUCKY PENNY

In the world of NASCAR, it seemed that Dale Earnhardt had done just about everything in his 23 years as a driver. In Winston Cup races, Dale won the pole position 22 times, had 70 first place finishes, and by the end of the 1997 season, won seven Winston Cup Championships (tied with Richard Petty for the most ever).

It seemed as though he had done it all.

It only seemed that way.

There was one thing Dale had not accomplished in his career. It was the only conquest he had yet to conquer. It was the crowned jewel of stock car racing...the Daytona 500. He had come so close so many times that he could almost taste it. In 19 trips to Daytona, Dale finished in the top five 10 times, and came in second-place 4 times (another record).

It seemed that one of the greatest drivers in auto racing history might have to retire one day amidst whispers about the one that got away.

It only seemed that way.

On Saturday, February 14, 1998 Dale Earnhardt met a 7-year-old girl from Phyllis, Kentucky, named Wessa Miller. Wessa, who used a wheelchair, was in Daytona to meet Earnhardt and attend the race courtesy of the Make-A-Wish Foundation. The little girl pulled a penny from her pocket and gave it to Dale saying "this is going to win you the Daytona 500." The next day, just before the race, Earnhardt taped the penny to the dashboard of his #3 Chevrolet.

The rest is auto racing history. Dale finally captured the one thing that had eluded him throughout his career. Dale Earnhardt won the Daytona 500. Earnhardt's helmet, racing gloves and car (complete with penny) went on display at NASCAR's museum next door. Wessa and her family went home to Kentucky and opened up a new restaurant. They called it 'The Lucky Penny'.

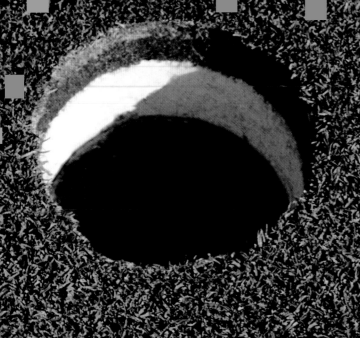

POCKET MONEY

The superstition of carrying around a lucky coin is believed to have started around 560 B.C. by the Lydians, the first people to mint coins. The early coins were often inscribed with spiritual inscriptions and mystical symbols causing people prone to superstition to see them as good-luck pieces, hence, they began to carry the coins everywhere they went.

Coin superstitions still thrive today. When someone makes a gift of a knife, it is believed important to give them a penny along with it, lest they want to sever the relationship. In the case the gift is a purse, coins are tucked inside so the owner may never be without money. Many people consider heads-up pennies found on the ground to be lucky and worth taking.

The list goes on and on.

Athletes, never to miss out on a mojo-opportunity, are big-league believers in toting around various coinages during competition. Former Atlanta Falcons™ tight end Jim Mitchell taped pennies to his cleats before every game. Cy Young Award™ winner Vida Blue carried two dimes in his back pocket in the hopes of luring a 20-win season. Golfers, however, take the prize for most 'mojo-conscious' when it comes to coins.

Even the titans of the game, while seemingly unflappable and cool as they tap in putts worth thousands of dollars, are carrying coins of various size, worth and origin to help their cause. Maybe the old adage "It takes money to make money" motivates Charles Coody to carry the British half-penny his daughter gave him, or Hale Irwin to tote around a Japanese coin with a hole in the middle. Jack Nicklaus and Tom Weiskopf each quietly carry three pennies with them every round, unlike Chi Chi Rodriguez, one of golf's most charismatic personalities, who prefers to spread his mojo-money all over the green for everyone to see. Among the lucky coins Chi Chi carries in his pocket during rounds are: a quarter to mark his ball before putting for birdies; a buffalo nickel to mark par and eagle putts; and a gold piece, just in case the mojo in the other coins gets used up.

Before the start of the Detroit Grand Prix in 1996, Paul Newman, gourmet popcorn afficionado, salad dressing king, Academy Award winning actor and co-owner of Newman-Haas Racing, approached his driver Christian Fittipaldi, nephew of Brasilian racing legend Emerson, handed him a quarter and explained that he was paying off a bet. Christian promptly zipped his newly acquired quarter safely into his suit and ran his best race of the season. Fittipaldi battled from 6th place to 1st, where he was leading with 6 laps to go when teammate Michael Andretti passed him for the win. While Newman was obviously pleased with the first/second place finish for his drivers, he was elated with Fittipaldi's marked improvement. Not to diminish Christian's driving skills, Newman, in true locker room mojo style, credited the quarter with an assist on the day.

From then on, the whole team kept a watchful eye on the lucky coin. Fittipaldi was often grilled as to the coin's whereabouts as he climbed into his car before a race.

During the time trials preceding the 1997 Australian Grand Prix, Fittipaldi was on fire. He ran his car like a man possessed. With the quarter nestled safely inside his racing suit, Christian posted some of his best qualifying times ever. He was running so well that his teammate, Michael Andretti, predicted that Christian would win the Grand Prix the next day.

It was not to be.

On the second lap of the race another driver, Gil de Ferran, hit Fittipaldi from behind, sending him head-on into the wall at 180 miles per hour.

Later, as Newman lamented that the quarter was not lucky afterall, Fittipaldi reluctantly confessed to leaving the coin in his hotel room by mistake.

The Lucky Quarter

THE COIN TOSS

In the early days, ballplayers believed that to see a funeral procession passing by was an omen of the worst sort. It was a message that their fortunes were about to take a very dark turn. There was only one course of action to be taken that would reverse the mojo back in their favor, but it had to be done immediately. Whoever observed the funeral procession would have to flip a coin in the direction of the deceased while they were still in view. By doing this, the curse would be removed and the mojo meter set right again.

Coin-tossing to settle a controversy is a popular custom which dates back as far as the time of Julius Caesar, whose likeness was engraved on one side of all coins minted during his reign as emperor of Rome (circa 100–44 b.c.). When an argument ensued, a coin was flipped, and if Caesar's head showed, whoever chose heads was right and the argument was settled.

During his playing days in the NFL, Stan Jones, former All-Pro guard with the Chicago Bears, was involved in one of the more mojo-tinged coin-tosses on record. As offensive captain, it was Jones' responsibility, along with the Bears' defensive captain, Bill George, to participate in the official pre-game coin-toss to determine which team would kickoff or receive the ball. One of the coaches alerted Jones to the fact that George, an All-Pro middle linebacker, was deadly superstitious about getting back to the sidelines first after the coin toss. Naturally, Jones decided he would have to beat him back to the sidelines the very next game.

The whole team was in on it. As the coin was tossed into the air, Jones reached across and quickly shook hands with the opposing captains, then sprinted for the sidelines. George saw what he was doing, quickly shook hands, and took off as fast as he could. The Bears were lined up screaming and cheering as Jones reached the sideline first. The home crowd was up on its feet yelling like crazy. "I guess they figured we were sky high for the game." Jones concluded.

Food for Thought...

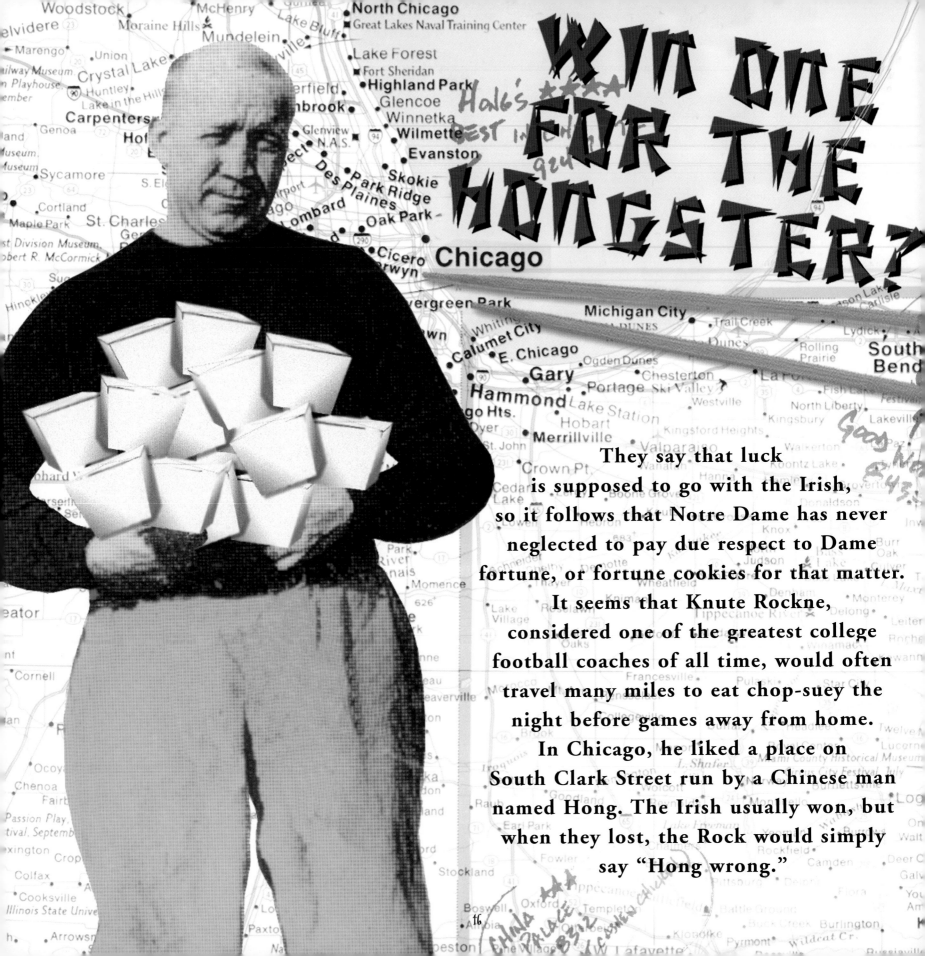

WIN ONE FOR THE HONGSTER?

They say that luck is supposed to go with the Irish, so it follows that Notre Dame has never neglected to pay due respect to Dame fortune, or fortune cookies for that matter. It seems that Knute Rockne, considered one of the greatest college football coaches of all time, would often travel many miles to eat chop-suey the night before games away from home. In Chicago, he liked a place on South Clark Street run by a Chinese man named Hong. The Irish usually won, but when they lost, the Rock would simply say "Hong wrong."

46

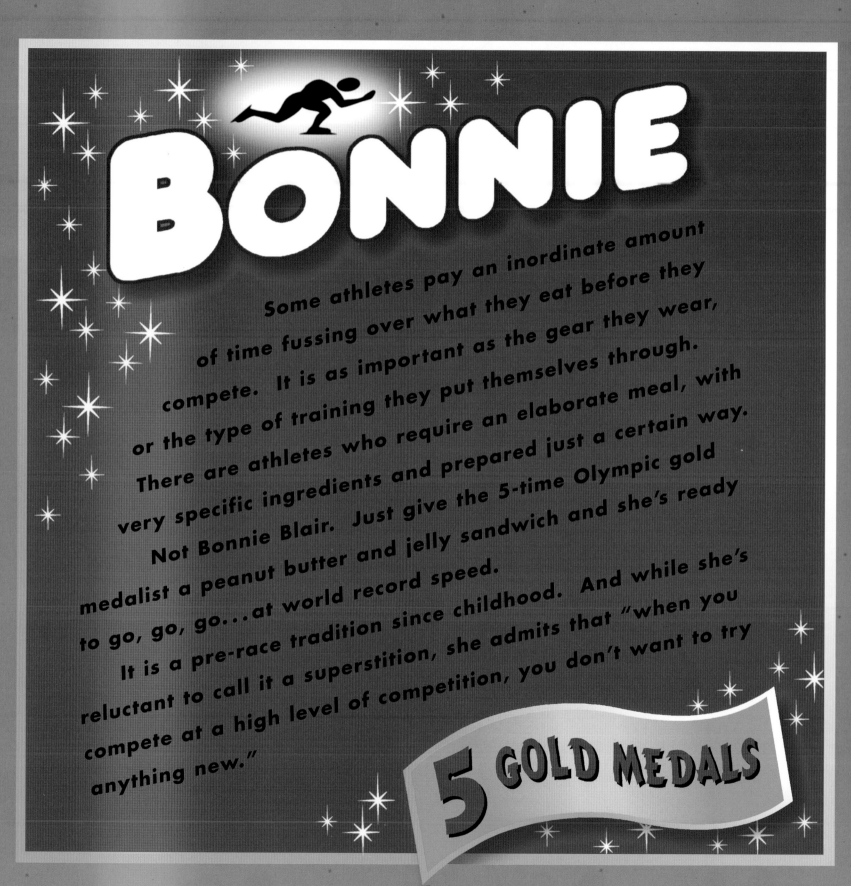

BONNIE

Some athletes pay an inordinate amount of time fussing over what they eat before they compete. It is as important as the gear they wear, or the type of training they put themselves through. There are athletes who require an elaborate meal, with very specific ingredients and prepared just a certain way.

Not Bonnie Blair. Just give the 5-time Olympic gold medalist a peanut butter and jelly sandwich and she's ready to go, go, go...at world record speed.

It is a pre-race tradition since childhood. And while she's reluctant to call it a superstition, she admits that "when you compete at a high level of competition, you don't want to try anything new."

5 GOLD MEDALS

THE PEANUT PRINCIPLE

Behold, The Mighty Peanut. The seemingly innocuous vegetable enjoyed worldwide as the standard snack choice at parties and sporting events. The food stuff whose taste is so beloved that its flavor is imitated in everything from cookies to milkshakes, is generally a very underated food.

Not, however, in the world of auto racing.

Four-time Indy 500 winner Rick Mears refuses to allow peanuts near the cockpit of his Marlboro Penske Chevy. Rick Galles, owner of the Valvoline and Molson Chevys of Al Unser Jr. and Danny Sullivan, respectively, chooses which candies are allowed in the pit and garage areas. Peanuts are off-limits.

Why is this sumptuous mini-snack so dreaded and unwelcome in a world generally associated with nerves of steel?

HERE'S WHAT WE FOUND

The origin of the bad reputation the peanut suffers in and around the race world stems from a horrible accident which occurred during a dirt track race in the late 1930's. The car was demolished and the driver severely injured. The subsequent investigation into the cause of the accident was narrowed down to a certain engine part where they discovered, you guessed it, a peanut.

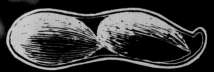

PEANUT
Arachis hypogaea

It's generally believed that some key ingredients
to a successful career as a professional athlete in any sport are
perserverance, perspiration and practice, practice, practice.
Some athletes, however, tend to sprinkle in a little secret ingredient of
their own. A little mojo spice to help in their endeavor to succeed.

St. Louis slugger Steve Bilko absolutely had to eat at least one candy bar
before every game. While Steve Preece, safety for the Seattle
Seahawks™, felt his recipe for success needed a pinch more sugar.
Well, maybe a handful. On game day, following breakfast,
Preece would eat one candy bar every hour on the hour until game time.

Steve's list of ingredients was specific, either Hershey's chocolate bars,
or, more appropriate to the coming task at hand, he would eat
Nestle's Crunch.

The counter in the proverbial mojo-diner is a crowded one. Almost every athlete has a food ritual or superstition of some sort. A certain, specific dish prepared a certain, specific way, and sometimes...eaten at a certain, specific time.

The reasons are as varied as the foods themselves. Some athletes are simply looking for that perfect nutritional edge, intent on filling their finely tuned bodies with the proper fuel for optimal performance. Like NASCAR great Darrell Waltrip's desire to load up on potassium by eating two bananas before each race.

Other, more mojo-conscious warriors, feel the need to eat the same meal every day as long as they are performing well. Pittsburgh Pirates™ great Al Lopez ate kippered herring and eggs for breakfast 17 days in a row during a hitting streak. Baltimore's Jim Palmer religiously ate pancakes while he was winning on the mound. Asked if he might consider changing his diet, Palmer explained, "I went 17-2 during one streak eating pancakes, so why take a chance?"

Hall of Famer Tommy Lasorda was probably as well known around Los Angeles for his love of Italian cuisine as he was for the 2 World Championships, 4 National League™ pennants, and eight Western Division Titles his Los Angeles Dodgers™ won during the 20 years he was manager.

Lasorda always ate linguine before a game. He would have red clam sauce if the team were facing a right-handed pitcher — and white, if they were facing a 'lefty'.

EATING DIS ORDER

TODAY'S LINE-UP

50

Pardon My Ectoplasm...

GHOST RIDER

DURING HIS HEYDAY, CELEBRATED JOCKEY FRED ARCHER WAS REGULARLY SEEN AT NEWMARKET RACE COURSE, USUALLY WINNING RACES.

THESE DAYS, ARCHER MAY STILL BE SEEN ON OCCASION AT NEWMARKET MOUNTED ATOP HIS FAVORITE GRAY. THE DIFFERENCE IS THAT FRED ARCHER HAS BEEN DEAD FOR MORE THAN ONE HUNDRED YEARS.

SOMETIME DURING 1886, ARCHER, IN A MOMENT OF DESPAIR, TOOK HIS OWN LIFE. SINCE THEN, HIS GHOST IS SAID TO BE ACCOUNTABLE FOR MANY UNEXPLAINED ACCIDENTS DURING RACES WHEN HORSES STUMBLE OR FLOUNDER FOR NO APPARENT REASON.

WHILE LEAVING THE TRACK A FEW YEARS AGO, TWO WOMEN REPORTED SEEING A RATHER STRANGE LOOKING JOCKEY RIDING TOWARDS THEM. THEY LATER IDENTIFIED THE RIDER AS ARCHER FROM A PORTRAIT HANGING IN THE CLUBHOUSE.

Lady of the Links

For those who play the game, golf can be a frightening enough proposition all on its own. There's the fear of getting safely off that first tee. The fear of the sand, the water, the woods. The fear of catching the shanks, or forgetting the lesson that cured them when you had them. The fear of the inevitable emergency that always occurs in the office when you finally get to take the day off. Fear is a part of the dynamic of golf. It drives the marketplace. All of the thousands of video tapes, handbooks and specially engineered clubs are designed to speak to that fear, and suppress it, if only temporarily.

For those who play the game at the Upminster Golf Club, golf can be a terrifying experience. The club is haunted.

In the very early morning hours, the apparition of a woman has been seen gliding about the grounds. There one moment, then at once, gone. "Personally, I've not seen her," explains Upminster's manager John Collantine, "but plenty of members and staff have. They call her Mary."

Years ago, when the clubhouse was torn apart for reconstruction, a woman's skeleton was found in one of the building's walls. Whether or not Mary met with an untimely end leaving her with an uncompleted round with this life is unknown. Some suggest that she may indeed be the first golf widow.

Upminster Golf Club

COMPETITION					Membership No.	Handicap	Strokes Rec'd	Please indicate which tee used		✔
DATE 8/28		TIME 2:45 pm						PAR 69 / SSS 69		✓
					515	12		PAR 69 / SSS 68		
Player A Dennis						7		PAR 71 / SSS 71		
Player B Gean							Nett 53 Score	W=+ L=- H=0 Points	Red Yards	Par	Stroke Index
Hole	Marker's	White	Par	Yellow Yards	Stroke Index	Score A	B		151	3	15

The Goal Digger

"Dorothy", the resident ghost of the Hockey

Hall of fame in Toronto, actually pre-dates the Hall

itself. In fact, she came with the building, the historic

Bank of Montreal building on the corner of front and

Yonge Streets in downtown Toronto.

Legend has it that "Dorothy" was a teller at the bank

back in 1910 and had an affair with the bank manager

to get closer to the money.

Nowadays, quite naturally, "Dorothy"

hangs around hockey's crown jewel, the

Stanley Cup™.

Sports fans come in many shapes and sizes. From the ambivalent fan who leaves the game in the eighth inning regardless of the score to avoid the annoying post-game traffic, to the fanatical fan who will gladly strip half-naked, paint themselves in their beloved team's colors, and stand from kick-off to final gun in sub-zero temperatures.

While he won't be seen with 'war-paint' on his face, or waving a giant foam finger, Fred M. Vinson is one the greats among the legions of the truly faithful football fans. Fred will arrive early and stay late no matter what the score is. No matter how harsh the weather may be. Fred is there for the duration.

Vinson has rarely missed a home football game at his alma mater, Centre College, in over 40 years. Which is really impressive considering Vinson died in 1953.

A former Chief Justice of the U.S. Supreme Court and graduate of Centre College's Class of 1909, Vinson is the most revered member of the Phi Delta Theta fraternity at Centre. On game days ever since his death, Vinson's fraternity brothers take his portrait down from it's sacred spot in the Phi Delta house, and escort his image to the game.

His frat brothers show due respect referring to the man as Mr. Vinson, but they simply, and affectionately call the portrait 'Dead Fred'.

Dead Fred

REMAINS OF THE DAY

Ah, cruel death,

why were you

so unkind?

To take Sir Dan

and leave

such trash behind

- Eulogy to Dan Donnelly, 1820

It is said that good luck will surely follow those who follow the footsteps of Dan Donnelly. And follow them you may. Two rows of carefully preserved indentations in the grass are visible leading away from a stone monument, up a hill towards the town of Kilcullen in the county Kildare, just south of Dublin. It was on this sacred piece of Irish soil, known as the Curragh, December 13th, 1815, that boxer Dan Donnelly wrote a page in Irish history by beating the English champ George Cooper.

The ninth of 17 children born to a dockhand's family, Donnelly was discovered while brawling with a local bully and turned into a professional prize-fighter by a promoter named Captain Kelly.

A sacred spot on the Curragh.

By the time he met Cooper on the Curragh, Donnelly was already a legend throughout all of Ireland.

There was much more than a £60 purse at stake in the contest. The fight was a matter of national honor. It was the year 1815 and Ireland was a nation suffering under the oppressive rule of Britain's mad King George III. Ireland was still licking her wounds from a failed Catholic uprising of 17 years past.

Donnelly was knocked down, and nearly out, in the second round, but rallied to win in dramatic fashion in the 11th round. The big Irishman had broken Cooper's jaw and defeated a nation with the same blow.

All of Ireland was grateful.

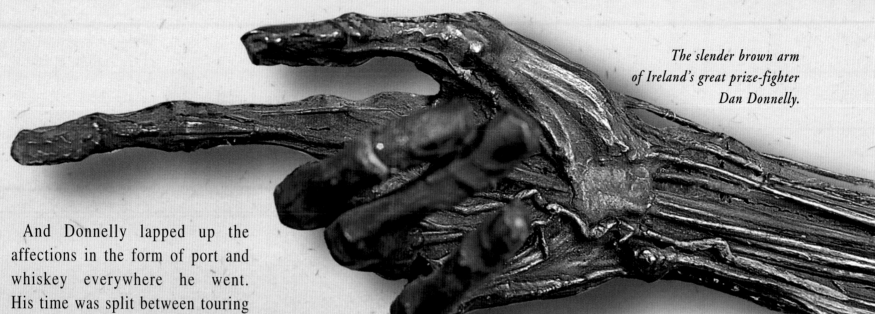

The slender brown arm of Ireland's great prize-fighter Dan Donnelly.

And Donnelly lapped up the affections in the form of port and whiskey everywhere he went. His time was split between touring the countryside as the Champion of Ireland, and operating various drinking establishments. Sadly, it was his penchant for drink that did him in. Five years after his historic victory over George Cooper, Dan Donnelly was dead at the age of 32.

The city of Dublin mourned their hero with a funeral the likes of which were usually reserved for a head of state. Dan was laid to rest on the grounds of the Royal Hospital in Kilmainham.

But not for long.

This was 1820, and grave-robbing was a booming industry. Surgeons paid dearly for cadavers to use in medical education. So rampant was this trade, it became necessary for the graves of the recently departed to be guarded night and day.

It was Donnelly's misfortune that he should die in the winter. Of the faithful who were charged with standing watch at his grave

Des Byrne proudly displays his fistic relic.

Carrick's Morning Post of February 23rd, 1820 reported: *Their naturally jovial disposition, and the severity of the weather prompted them to make too frequent libations on the tomb of* *the departed champion and disabled them from perceiving or opposing those riflers of the House of Death.*

Donnelly's body was brought to a surgeon named Hall, who upon recognizing the famous corpse brought before him, demanded they immediately return him to his grave. But first, he grabbed a hacksaw and detached the once-feared right arm of Ireland's most famous pugilist.

Since 1820, the arm was used in anatomy lessons at Edinburgh University, on exhibit in a traveling circus, and displayed in a pub, ironically named the Duncain Arms. It was purchased in 1953 by Jim Byrne, and handed down to son Des, proud keeper of Dan's arm, and legend to date.

By the end of the first decade of this century, baseball's popularity was like a rising fastball. Ever-increasing crowds stuffed ballparks beyond capacity to see players like Ty Cobb, and Christy Mathewson, the new baseball stars of the modern age. And new and bigger ballparks were rising up to facilitate those crowds. Comiskey Park, Ebbets Field, Fenway Park, just three of the eleven new parks that were built between 1909 and 1915, Braves Field in Boston being the last.

The Boston Braves™ deserved a new home. After all, in 1914 they won the World Series™ in a four game sweep of Philadelphia. What they got was more than they bargained for.

During construction of the new 'Braves Field', an area of the playing field gave way and opened into a gaping sink hole. Workmen, wagons, and animals plunged into a 20-foot chasm. The men were pulled to safety. But it was an impossible task to lift out the badly injured horses and mules. The crew had no choice but to shoot the animals and spare them from further misery.

THEY SHOOT HORSES ...DON'T THEY?

The dead beasts were covered up with the dirt needed to fill the huge hole.

In time, most everyone forgot about the giant sink hole and the death-dealing cave-in.

But when the Braves continued to lose season after season - they finished fifth or lower in 26 of the 38 years they played at 'Braves Field' - fans began to wonder if somehow the buried horses and mules were to blame.

A medium claimed she picked up a psychic message from the spirits of the dead animals which declared that the Braves would be cursed for as long as they played on the equine graves.

The medium was right. The team never won another world championship while playing at that park.

It wasn't until 1957, five years after they moved to Milwaukee, that the Braves won their next World Series.

Makes you wonder how many horses are buried in Wrigley Field.

Percy Lambert

The Brooklands race circuit in Weybridge - Surrey, England, may well be considered the 'Kittyhawk' of British motorsport. After all, it was here on the world's oldest race track on February 15, 1913, that Percy Lambert became the first person in the world to reach the 100 miles-per-hour mark in an automobile. An achievement considered one of the greatest accomplishments in early motorsport.

Brooklands, known as the 'birthplace of motor racing and aviation', is now a museum situated on 30 sanctified acres where tribute is paid to the legendary pioneers who designed, built and raced the cars, motorbikes and aircraft here. And if you believe the stories, some of them are still around

At night, it is said, Brooklands' old aircraft hangar, clubhouse and long-abandoned engineer sheds are fraught with the restless spirits of those who met untimely ends here. The most famous specter on these hallowed grounds is that of Percy Lambert's. His apparition is said to appear out of the early morning mist on the Members' banking of the old race circuit where he fatally crashed only eight months after breaking the 100 mph barrier.

On October 31, 1913, Lambert was driving in what he had promised his fiancee would be his last race. The 103 mph record Percy had established that previous February was quickly broken by another driver, and he wanted one more shot at regaining it before he retired. During his run, Lambert was out of sight on the Member's banking when a loud bang was heard. When the race marshals rushed to the site they found Lambert's car had rolled down the embankment and Percy found slumped against a tree. A burst tire is thought to have caused the accident.

Percy Lambert died on the way to Weybridge Cottage Hospital on Halloween Day, 1913, a week before he was due to be married.

Percy Lambert in the Talbot Pearley 3 at Brooklands Race Circuit, 1913.

A crowd of spectators cheer the racers on as they enter the Member's Banking, where Percy met his untimely end.

Something Wicket This Way Comes

Motorists near the town of Markyate, England, have often times been startled to see the ghostly figures of two young men standing along the roadside where, in 1958, a bus ferrying a cricket team home from a match was involved in an accident that proved fatal to two of the teams' members.

By the time friendly drivers pull over to offer the young men a ride, they vanish.

Fashion Forward...

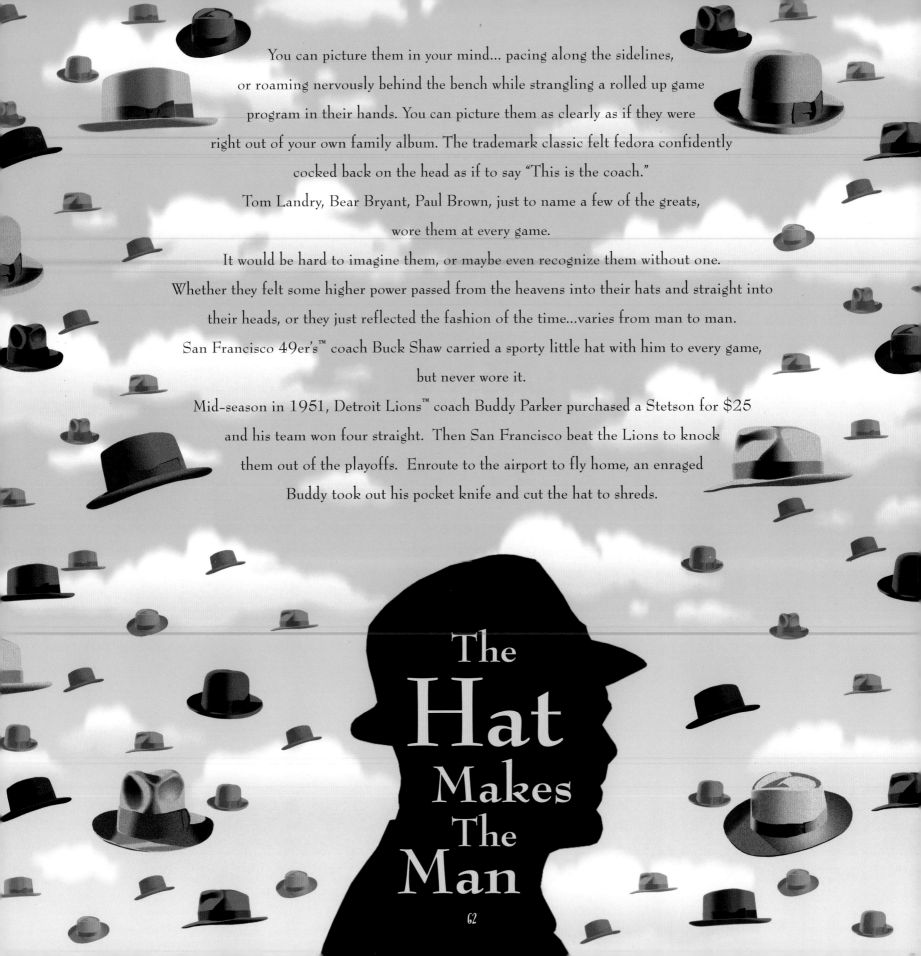

You can picture them in your mind... pacing along the sidelines,
or roaming nervously behind the bench while strangling a rolled up game
program in their hands. You can picture them as clearly as if they were
right out of your own family album. The trademark classic felt fedora confidently
cocked back on the head as if to say "This is the coach."
Tom Landry, Bear Bryant, Paul Brown, just to name a few of the greats,
wore them at every game.
It would be hard to imagine them, or maybe even recognize them without one.
Whether they felt some higher power passed from the heavens into their hats and straight into
their heads, or they just reflected the fashion of the time...varies from man to man.
San Francisco 49er's™ coach Buck Shaw carried a sporty little hat with him to every game,
but never wore it.
Mid-season in 1951, Detroit Lions™ coach Buddy Parker purchased a Stetson for $25
and his team won four straight. Then San Francisco beat the Lions to knock
them out of the playoffs. Enroute to the airport to fly home, an enraged
Buddy took out his pocket knife and cut the hat to shreds.

The
Hat
Makes
The
Man

IT SUITS HIM WELL

Hockey players, coaches and owners have so many superstitions that they tend to tilt the Mojo Meter to the extreme levels. And two of the game's true immortals are tied to what turned out to be a rather expensive, unwieldy but ultimately splendidly sartorial bit of superstitition. It is something that gives direct refutation to the belief that guys involved with hockey are the least stylish - clothing wise - than their peers in football, basketball or baseball.

Scotty Bowman, who has a bag of Stanley Cups in his background - from Montreal, Pittsburgh and Detroit - was known to eat a pre-game meal in a lucky restaurant. And then he would return, again, and again, before every game, until the luck ran out. He would switch restaurants and start all over again. But, all of that paled in comparison to what Punch Imlach - who steered the Toronto Maple Leafs™ to four Stanley Cups between 1962 and 1967 --would do to give himself and his team that certain edge on the ice.

When Toronto Maple Leafs would go on the road to play the Montreal Canadiens, Imlach would ask close friends to go with him to a secret, special location. They were headed to, yes, Tony The Tailor.

Imlach needed that clothes-horse edge: He had to buy a lucky suit.

Of course, if the Maple Leafs won while Imlach donned his new threads, it caused a bit of a problem. Imlach believed that he had to go back and buy another suit before the next game. According to people close to Imlach, he had a very large wardrobe. Obviously his suit collection - and Tony The Tailor's bank account - grew in direct proportion to those glorious, championship years enjoyed by Imlach and the Toronto Maple Leafs.

A BLANKET STATEMENT

Old-time boxers were known as a particularly superstitious bunch. Almost every one of the greats, from Jake LaMotta to Joe Louis, had certain things they believed in, trusted and resorted to. Former welterweight champion Jimmy McLarnin was on the receiving end of somebody else's Aromatic Mojo - and he didn't like it one bit at all. One of McLarnin's regular opponents was a jabbing, hard-nosed pugilist with a classic nickname: Billy "Fargo Express" Petrolle. Billy decided that he would never enter the ring unless he had a special Native American blanket draped over his shoulders. The blanket was an old, unwashed and crumbling item. It was also very lucky for Petrolle - he refused to get rid of it, even when other boxers and managers were complaining about it. In just the same way that basketball immortal Pete Maravich treated his socks, Petrolle refused to wash his blanket. That act, of course, would rinse away whatever accumulated Mojo had been built up over the years. The problem was that his refusal to clean the blanket left it smelling a little pungent. Call it the Aromatic Mojo. Call it what you want, but welterweight champ

McLarnin was convinced that the smell of the blanket had a more powerful knockout punch than anything he had ever seen. "That thing smelled so bad that it almost chloroformed his opponents, me included," he said. The first time the two fought, Petrolle beat the pants off of McLarnin. And, of course, it was also the first time that McLarnin got his initial whiff of the smelly blanket. Next two times out, McLarnin knew what was coming. He steered clear of the blanket -

and the Aromatic Mojo. Those next two times, McLarnin was able to beat Petrolle.

In the great 'mojo wardrobe', the tie is one of the most called upon articles of clothing by an athlete or coach when looking for a fashion edge to enhance their performance.

It could be that ties need to be cleaned less often, enabling the wearer to keep it on indefinitely, if necessary, without attracting attention. Unlike those who refuse to change, or wash suits as long as they keep winning, ultimately offending anyone within whiffing distance.

Lynn "Pappy" Waldorf, legendary football coach of the University of California, coached his Golden Bears to three straight Rose Bowl appearances in 1949, '50 and '51 wearing his cardinal and gold tie to every game during that period.

But nobody benefited more, or more publicly, from a lucky tie than Leon "Red" Ames. Red was a right-hander for John McGraw's New York Giants™ from 1903 to 1913.

Throughout the 1908 season Red struggled. It seemed that no matter how well he pitched, he couldn't seem to win ballgames. On opening day in 1909 he pitched a brilliant game against Brooklyn, throwing a no-hitter through nine innings, only to lose the game in the thirteenth.

Game after game Red pitched like a master, losing by low scores due to an error by a teammate or because his team had not given him any offense. The press labeled Ames as the "hoodoo" pitcher, and called him the "man who couldn't win."

On the first stop of a long road trip, Ames received a package from a friend containing a four-leaf clover and a necktie. Directions on a note stated that in order for the four-leaf clover to work, it must be worn on both his uniform and street clothes, and the necktie must be worn with the street clothes and concealed under his uniform.

Concealing the necktie was easier said than done. It was so loud and colorful it made Bozo the Clown's costume look like funeral attire.

Red dutifully put the necktie on and tucked the four-leaf clover into his wallet.

The first game Red pitched in, he won handily. That night at dinner, he pointed to his necktie and said "I don't change her until I lose.' Red slept with the tie under his pillow every night from then on.

Everytime Red won a game, columns were printed in the papers about the necktie. It became the most famous tie in the world.

He didn't lose one game on that road trip. In fact, Red didn't lose until the last game of the season against Brooklyn. Ames blamed that loss on lack of support, citing John McGraw's decision to put some young talent into the lineup for what the manager considered a meaningless game.

According to Ames, it wasn't the tie's fault at all.

WORN TO PERFECTION

When it comes to mojo, there are prevalent threads that tend to abound - certain areas where the mojo monsters tend to appear more often. Those areas have to do with food, clothing and color. David Cone has a lucky leather jacket. Pete Maravich would wear his socks forever and ever, until they tended to look like droopy, melted Salvador Dali images hanging onto his magic ankles. Everybody in sports, it seems, has some little bit of clothing mantra, mojo, ritual - from being superstitious about the way their ankles are taped to wearing Babe Ruth's hat during a game (which is what New York Yankees,™ David Wells, who pitched one of baseball's rare perfect games in 1998, once did).

Vida Blue, the great left-hander for the Oakland Athletics™, had a lucky hat which he wore in every game for four straight years. It was old, funky and faded. And several American League™ umpires refused to let Vida take the mound wearing his gamey headpiece. But Blue persisted. He continued to wear it until he was ultimately threatened with a stiff fine and suspension from a game. Vida finally relented, but not before he ceremoniously burned the hat on the field before a game.

THE LUCKY RUG

I PREFER 'HAIR-PIECE' IF YOU DON'T MIND.

They say love sneaks up on you when you least expect it. But if you go looking for it, you rarely find it.

Luck is like that too. You never know where it might be. It could be just around the corner, or right under your nose.

Or, in Norm Sherry's case, on top of your head.

Back in 1977, the balding manager of the California Angels™ was making some extra cash doing television commercials for

a toupee company. With his new lid in place, Sherry masterminded his team to four straight wins.

Then, when the team took to the road, Norm left his 'mojo-rug' at home. The Angels lost four in a row.

While Sherry was anxious to get his hair-piece comfortably back on his head, his wife Mardie was in no hurry.

"She says it makes me look like Howard Cosell," Norm confessed.

BrING On DA' FuNK!

Refusing to wash a lucky t-shirt or pair of socks during a winning streak is among the most common of superstitions with athletes at all levels. But the Purdue Women's Rugby Club has taken that mojo to an all new malodorous high.

It seems as long long as they are winning, the whole uniform goes unwashed. With a roster of fourteen, these gals have proven there truly is strength in numbers.

Coach C. J. Jones came clean with the mojo citing, "If the luck is in the fabric, why risk washing it out?" Ok...but as the Lady Boilermaker's winning streak grows don't be surprised if the fan attendance shrinks.

The legion of faithful may prefer to revel in the team's success from the safety of the newspaper box scores the morning after.

Clothing makes the man. Clothing also protects the man. And nothing protects a man more - or more importantly - than his "groin protector." Sometimes known simply as a 'cup,' it has become an indispensable, though often unmentioned piece of equipment out on the field. It especially means a lot to someone in the field when they are faced with that chilling, frozen moment when a screaming line drive is bearing down on you at full supersonic speed and it is aimed right at a sensitive spot.

Jim Ohms, who played for the Daytona Beach Islanders in 1966, believed his protector was so lucky he had to make a major mojo investment in it. In the mid-1960's, he used to put a penny in the pouch of his supporter after each win. His teammates and opposing players were treated to the sound of pennies banging against the pitcher's plastic cup when he ran the bases or took the mound. No word what he would do if he had one of those rare 30-win seasons - or decided to stretch it over a lifetime and had the good fortune to win 300 games.

SAVING YOUR ASSETS

In the summer of '94, lefty Kenny Rogers was in the middle of what would turn out to be one of the most blissful, exquisite moments in sports — The Perfect Game. Little did he know how much his team-mates really wanted him to achieve utter perfection. They had embarked upon The Sacrifice of The Red Shoes.

While the Texas Rangers'™ left-hander uncorked one perfect pitch after another, two reserve players — Chris James and Gary Redus — had taken superstar Jose Canseco's battered red baseball shoes and dipped them in alcohol. Then, during the fifth inning, when it was pretty clear to everyone at the ballpark in Arlington that Rogers was on his way to something mighty special, they set fire to the shoes. In the middle of the dugout. With the rest of the Rangers still in the field. It was their Mojo — their way of making sure Rogers had his Perfect Game.

Will Clark was playing first and was stunned when he saw the explosion of flames. He started laughing when he realized they were burning some red shoes. So did the rest of the Rangers. So were the Mojo Gods — they decided that it was OK for Rogers to have his moment after all. The Mojo Gods were appeased.

Of course, Rogers never even noticed the red shoe inferno. Mojo works that way sometimes. It can be right in front of you — and pointing you to perfection — but you might never see it. Kenny Rogers pitched the 12th perfect game in modern baseball history.

A Tale From The Red Shoe Fieries

Whatever Works...

Just Ask The "Babe"

Get's The Red Out...
Won't Fill You Up!

ACME EYE WASH

One day during the New York Yankees™ 1930 season, Babe Ruth arrived at the ballpark with bloodshot eyes after a strenuous night. He asked the trainer "Watcha got to clear my eyes?" The trainer handed him a bottle of eye wash. Ruth put the wash in his eyes. He had three hits that day. The next six days, whether he needed it or not, Ruth used the eye wash and he made a hit everyday.

Then he went hitless.

Teammate Tony Lazzeri, who had been watching Ruth's treatment, bought a bottle of eye wash, emptied it, rinsed it and filled it with water. Then very conspicuously in front of Ruth, Lazzeri drank the whole bottle.

Ruth guffawed, "Look at the dumb guy," he said to the whole locker room,

"he drinks the eye wash."

That day Lazzeri got three hits.

Ruth was impressed. The next day he got a bottle of eye wash

from the trainer, downed the contents and remarked to Lazzeri

"Sure tastes terrible, doesn't it Tony?" But the Babe's batting streak resumed,

and he continued to drink the eye wash before every game as long as the string lasted.

Really-Works!

TOUCHED

DO NOT TOUCH STEFANO MODENA...NOT IF YOU WANT YOUR RACE TO START ON TIME.
THIS IS WHAT F.I.F.A. PRESIDENT JEAN MARIE BALESTRE FOUND OUT BEFORE THE START OF THE
BRASILIAN GRAND PRIX IN 1992.   AS THE CARS WERE REVVING THEIR ENGINES ON THE
STARTING GRID, PRES. BALESTRE WALKED IN BETWEEN THEM CASUALLY WISHING THE DRIVERS
GOOD FORTUNE WHEN HE LEANED DOWN AND TOUCHED STEFANO MODENA'S ARM.
UNBEKNOWNST TO BALESTRE, MODENA HAS A REAL THING ABOUT BEING TOUCHED ONCE
INSIDE THE COCKPIT OF HIS CAR. MODENA PROCEEDED TO UNSTRAP HIMSELF FROM THE
RACE CAR AND GET OUT. THEN HE GOT BACK IN, FASTENED HIS HARNESS, AND HIS RITUAL,
CLEAN AND UNADULTERATED BY HUMAN HANDS ONCE AGAIN, HE WAS READY TO RACE.

Whose Minding The Net?

Goalies, like catchers and sometimes punters, enjoy a special relationship with the Gods of Mojo. Maybe it's the fact that they have to blissfully stare down one wicked slap shot after another. Maybe it's the fact that they don't get to let off a little frustration by building up to some good G-force speeds out in the wide-open part of the ice. Maybe it's because they spend hours throwing themselves onto sticks and frozen water.

Whatever it is, guys like Pelle Lindbergh, the late, great goalie from the Philadelphia Flyers™, only added onto the mythology. Lindbergh had to wear an ancient orange T-shirt that came from, yes, Ingvar Eriksson's sporting-goods emporium in Stockholm. Each time it threatened to fall apart, he had someone sew it back together. Meantime, between periods, Lindbergh only allowed one thing to reach his lips – a Swedish beverage called Pripps. It didn't stop there: he wouldn't even taste it if there weren't exactly two ice cubes in the cup – a cup that had to, must, be delivered to him by a particular team trainer.

Ron Hextall, another Flyers' goalie, was known as a mighty slave to Mojo. The most noticeable moment was on the ice during timeouts. Fans and players would stop and stare as Hextall seemed to be beating up his goal post – once, twice, three times …eight times he would smack the post with his stick. Always eight times.
Not one more or less.

Lindbergh and Hextall were not alone in goalie Mojo Heaven. Patrick Roy has amused and amazed his faithful followers by insisting that when he speaks to the goal posts they will actually engage him in conversation.
Roy has an easy explanation for why he can hear the goal posts and no one else seems to: "They are my friends."

74

Magic Shoes

The horseshoe is at the center of many superstitions in cultures throughout history. Surprisingly, as symbols go, it represents only good luck. It is a positive talisman. It is a charm that invites favorable fortune. Simply put, it is great mojo.

The Greeks are believed to have invented the horseshoe sometime in the 4th century to, obviously, protect their horses' feet. The shoe was made with seven holes for nails - three on the outside, four on the inside - lucky number seven.

The Greeks nailed horseshoes to their walls as protection from the 'plague'. So did the Romans. Maybe even the Roman senators.

The Ottawa Senators™ did. They hung one over the door in their dressing room as protection from another kind of plague. The plague of losing hockey games.

According to team massage therapist Brad Joyal, someone sent the team two horseshoes. Joyal, being from western Canada, knew immediately what to do with them. "Back home, everybody has at least one hung over the door of their barn, or the front door of their house. I put velcro on the back of one and put it over the locker room door here at the Corel Centre."

The assistant equipment manager, "Woody" Gervais designated the other one to be their 'road shoe' and has placed a horseshoe over the door of every dressing room they inhabit on their road trips. It has been an integral part of their pre-game ritual. As the players file out of the room on their way to the ice, they touch, tap and rub the horseshoe. One player touches it once in the first period, two in the second, three in the third and four times if the game goes to overtime.

What's In a Number?

THE NUMBER 13 IS AN INTERNATIONAL SYMBOL OF BAD LUCK. NO 13TH FLOOR ELEVATORS (THOUGH THERE WAS A LEGENDARY PSYCHEDELIC BAND IN AUSTIN, TEXAS IN THE LATE 1960S THAT USED THAT VERY NAME), AND NOT A WHOLE LOT OF 13'S ON THE BACK OF UNIFORMS. SOMETHING ABOUT THE NUMBER SCARES AWAY THE VERY PEOPLE WHO SAY THAT THEY ARE NOT SCARED BY ANYTHING. SOMETHING ABOUT THE NUMBER CAUSES PEOPLE WHO DON'T NORMALLY WORRY ABOUT NUMBERS - OTHER THAN TO CHECK HOW MANY ASSISTS THEY HAVE BEEN DISHING OUT, HOW MANY INTERCEPTIONS THEY HAVE SKYJACKED, HOW MANY TDS THEY HAVE THROWN, WHAT THEIR HANDICAP IS OUT ON THE GOLF COURSE - SUDDENLY GET ALL SQUISHY AND CAUTIOUS WHEN IT COMES TO THE NUMBER 13.

IT IS BASIC LOCKER ROOM MOJO. IT IS ELEMENTAL LOCKER ROOM MOJO. IT IS THE GREAT EQUALIZER THAT WILL POP UP IN ALMOST ANY SETTING AT ANY TIME - AND IT IS ONE OF THE LOCKER ROOM MOJO ITEMS THAT GROWN MEN WILL OPENLY CONFESS TO WORRYING ABOUT. CALL IT FEAR - CALL IT TRISKAIDAPHOBIA, ITS CLINICAL NAME - BUT FROM STOCK CAR RACING TO HOCKEY, YOU WILL BE HARD PRESSED TO FIND ANYONE WHO EMBRACES THE NUMBER 13 AS THE LUCKIEST OF ALL NUMERICAL SYMBOLS. NO CAR WITH THE NUMBER 13 HAS BEEN ENTERED IN THE HALLOWED OF HOLIES - THE INDIANAPOLIS 500 - SINCE 1914. PLAYERS HAVE TRADED IN UNIFORMS WITH THE NUMBER ON IT, SAID SPECIAL PRAYERS WHEN THEY HAD TO PITCH ON THE 13TH DAY OF THE MONTH, AND GENERALLY HAVE STEERED CLEAR OF IT. MORE LIKE STAYED ON THE OTHER SIDE OF THE MOON WHENEVER THE UNLUCKY 13 MANIFEST ITSELF IN A SCORECARD, ON A JERSEY OR EVEN A LICENSE PLATE. BUT, OF COURSE, LIKE EVERYTHING IN LIFE, THERE ALWAYS HAS TO BE ONE EXCEPTION. THAT PERFECT MOMENT OF REVERSE LOCKER ROOM MOJO.

HERE IT IS:

WHEN RICK MACKEY WON THE IDITAROD TRAIL SLED DOG RACE IN 1983, HE WAS WEARING THE NUMBER 13. NOT ONLY THAT, HE WAS THE FIRST SON OF A FORMER IDITAROD CHAMPION TO ALSO WIN. HIS DAD'S WINNING NUMBER?

"13."

Sentinels of Speed

The Texas tandem of Terry and Bobby Labonte are folk heroes to the hundreds of thousands of racing fans across the country. Those ardent followers of motor sports will travel hundreds of miles to watch the Labonte boys in action - and sometimes will have to settle for a seat way in the back of a 150,000 seat speedway. From that faraway vantage point, they might have a hard time spotting Bobby's Tiny Fightin' Mojo.

Labonte likes to put a small plastic toy soldier on the dash of his souped-up Chevrolet Monte Carlo. The idea is that the little foot soldier can take aim at the track - and the rest of the racers that Labonte is going up against. The superstition started in 1995 after his pit crew began putting the toy soldiers in a tool box - as a way to protect the spark plugs. The soldiers were sent to the front line as a joke and then they wound up staying there after Labonte started winning.

All good troops need some backup.

Labonte also put a soldier in the back of his Monte Carlo. His mission: To protect the man from Corpus Christi, Texas from any and all advancing enemy. When Labonte has whipped the best drivers in the world - including Jeff Gordon in the Miller Genuine Draft 400 at Michigan International Speedway - the little toy soldiers were along for the ride. There is no word on whether the Members of the Mojo Military were wearing harnesses and racing helmets.

A SPITTING IMAGE

Tennis legend Martina Navaratilova was famous for her forehand, her iron-will and her

baseline-to-baseline slugfests with her friend and rival Chris Evert. That rivalry probably

did more than other to boost women's tennis into the big-time spotlight.

For a period, there was simply no more famous woman athlete than

Martina Navratilova. But, as recognizable as she was, there was a secret

slice of Mojo guiding her smashes, lobs and serves:

According to Martina there is an old Czech tradition that calls

for a friend or, especially, a family member to spit just behind

the ears. The great expectorations are supposed to bring

good luck to the person on the receiving end.

Martina, of course, cautioned that the best mojo

comes in moderation. "It's not really a spit.

You just make the noise," says Martina with a laugh.

Keeping it close to home, Martina preferred

that her mother Jana be the one who was letting

fly - or, hopefully, just making the noise.

You can't argue with Martina's Mojo -

she is, arguably, one of the three

greatest women tennis players

of all time.

Mental preparation. It is fundamental to any athlete's pre-competition ritual. What, where and how it is achieved is vastly different for each athlete. Most rituals are intensely private, personal, known only to the athlete, his teammates and maybe his family.

Jamie Storr for instance, netminder for the Los Angeles Kings™, puts on all his heavy gear, lays on the locker room floor, closes his eyes and begins to visualize all the various shots he will inevitably face in the coming game. During his visualization, his legs and arms perform a symphony of slow deliberate movements, denying the imaginary puck at every turn. When his fellow Kings first got a glimpse of the 'floor-show' they chided and kidded him. Now they simply step over him as they wend their way around the locker room, accepting Jamie's preparation as fixed scenery in their own pre-game world.

Some other athlete's rituals are harder

GETTING READY

to hide, becoming part of the public domain. When fearsome linebacker Jack "Hacksaw" Reynolds played on the road with the L.A. Rams, he would rise four hours before the rest of his team, eat his pre-game meal and go to the stadium long before his teammates, in order to properly prepare himself for the game. When Jack signed with the San Fransisco 49ers™, they did things differently. They held pre-game meetings at the hotel, then one more at the stadium before the game. In order to compensate for his lost prep-time, Jack had the equipment manager deliver his uniform to the hotel room, where he would completely suit up. Dressed for battle, "Hacksaw" would sprint past housekeeping, elude the rolling room service carts and burst into the lobby where he would join his team. After attending meetings and chapel, Jack would file out of the hotel and onto the team bus along side his street-clothed teammates, his tailor-made ritual out in the open for all the world to see.

"Charley"

John McGraw, manager of the New York Giants™ from 1902 to 1932, was one of the toughest competitors in the history of baseball. As a player, he was a 'go-through-the-wall' kind of guy. He knew no fear, and he brawled often. As manager, McGraw would do anything for his players, and try almost anything to win. John McGraw was an intensely superstitious man. He would quickly snatch up a penny or hairpin off the ground and stowe it away in his pocket in hopes that it had some good mojo left in it. And if a player had a strong superstition, McGraw would do whatever was necessary to facilitate it (see 'Roll Out The Barrells').

So when a thirty-year-old farmer named Charles Faust approached John McGraw on July 29, 1911, in the Planter's Hotel in St. Louis announcing that a fortune teller said Faust would become a great pitcher if he joined New York Giants, McGraw didn't hesitate to give him a tryout. Faust was terrible. McGraw and the team ditched him in St. Louis, but a couple of weeks later Charley caught up with the team in New York. He hung around for a couple of days and the Giants began to win. McGraw gave Charley a uniform and sat him on the bench. Every day he told him he would pitch. The Giants won three consecutive pennants with Charley on their bench. McGraw finally let Charley Faust pitch two meaningless innings in which he gave up two hits and two runs. Faust left the team in 1914, and the heavily favored Giants lost the pennant. Charles Victor Faust died in an asylum June 18, 1915.

Charles Victor Faust
New York Giants - Mascot

SAILING AWAY

Sailors, from the time of Odysseus right up to the quest for the America's Cup, have always sought some extra edge on the high seas. One of the oldest bits of Watery Mojo is found in the world of Olympic sailing:

Sailors believe that a practice race is one that you should never, ever, win. Crossing the finish line in a practice run is considered the highest form of bad luck and captain Skip Whyte knows all about it. In 1976, he was considered to be on the extremely short list for the United States squad that was headed for the Montreal Olympics. He made the rash, bad, mistake of winning one of his warm-up races. Whyte missed the final cut for the Olympic team by the narrowest of margins.

Four years later, he had learned his lesson. In a series of practice runs, he and other American sailors who seemed destined to win their warm-up races, decided to pull hard away from the finish line at the last possible second. Time after time, as the sailboats headed to a sure victory, the captains would tug on the tiller and make abrupt turns before crossing the winner's line.

FINISH LINE

Whyte explained it this way to a reporter from Boston: "You use up all your luck before it really counts."

IN SOME INDIGENOUS CULTURES, TO TAKE A PERSON'S PICTURE WAS CONSIDERED TABOO. IT WAS A NASTY OMEN OF THE HIGHEST ORDER. BAD MOJO TO THE EXTREME.

THE BELIEF WAS THAT A PERSON'S SOUL WOULD BE CAPTURED IN THE PICTURE... TAKING IT AWAY FROM THEM FOREVER.

THIS COULD BE WHY CHER, SEAN PENN, ALEC BALDWIN, AND SO MANY OF TODAY'S CELEBRITIES ARE SO SKITTISH AND EDGY AROUND THE PAPPARAZZI AND THEIR WARM, WINNING WAYS.

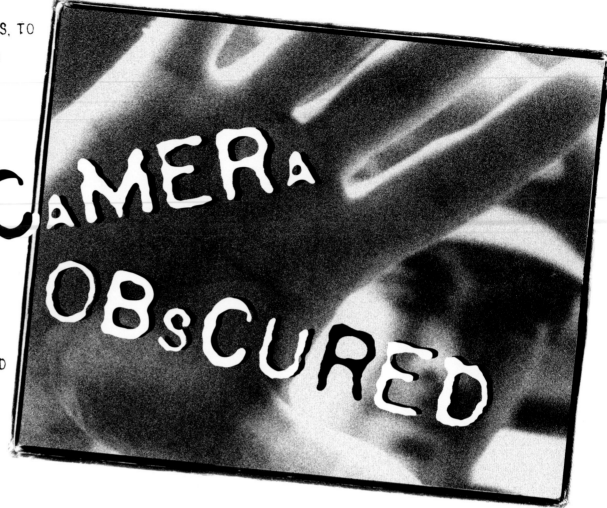

CAMERA OBSCURED

THEY'RE PROBABLY AFRAID OF JOINING THE GROWING LEGIONS OF 'SOULESS' ENTITIES ALREADY ROAMING HOLLYWOOD.

IN BASEBALL, PITCHERS HAVE BEEN KNOWN TO BE CAMERA SHY. BROOKLYN'S HUGH CASEY AND YANKEE HURLER VIC RASCHI FLATLY REFUSED TO HAVE THEIR IMAGE SNAPPED BEFORE A GAME IN WHICH THEY WERE PITCHING. NO ONE IN BASEBALL, HOWEVER, WAS MORE SENSITIVE ABOUT CAMERAS THAN ALBERT "CHIEF" BENDER. THE PITCHING ACE FOR THE PHILADELPHIA ATHLETICS[tm] FROM 1903 TO 1914, WAS A FULL-BLODDED

CHIPPEWA INDIAN AND AS TENDER AS A RAW NERVE WHEN IT CAME TO THE SUBJECT.

WHILE WARMING UP BEFORE ONE OF THE FIVE WORLD SERIES THE "CHIEF" APPEARED IN, A PHOTOGRAPHER SNAPPED HIS PICTURE. ENRAGED, BENDER GRABBED THE MAN AND PROMPTLY SNAPPED HIS CAMERA... IN HALF. NO TELLING WHETHER BENDER'S ATTACK ON THE CAMERAMAN CAME FROM A DEEP TRIBAL BELIEF, OR IF HE HAD JUST HAD ENOUGH OF HIS WARM WINNING WAYS.

Maybe it's the history of the game. Maybe it's the pace of the game, the way the mind can wander over the course of a long contest or a really long season. Whatever it is, baseball players have devised any number of ways to explore the inner recesses of mojo - and many of them have boiled it all down to the simple art of putting one foot in front of the other.

Walking . . . the way you do it, when you do it and where you do it . . . is as much a part of baseball mojo as anything else.

Babe Ruth always touched first base on his way into the dugout from right field. Joe Medwick used to touch third base on his way to the outfield. Joe DiMaggio also liked to touch first base when he was crossing the field. Mickey Mantle always touched first or third when he ran out to centerfield.

That's not all.

Jackie Robinson would stroll in front of the catcher on his way to the batter's box. And, if a pitcher and catcher decided to have a little meeting on the mound, Robinson liked to wait them out inside the on-deck circle.

Of coure, there was always the mighty king of the malaprop, Yogi Berra. Yogi made a cardinal rule of not turning around when he threw away his practice bats as he approached the batter's box. With Yogi's ability to make words wander all over the place, it's pure luck that his bats didn't do the same - and that one of them didn't wind up knocking out one of his team-mates.

LUCKY DETOUR

Puck O' The Irish

The four-leaf clover is probably the most popular good luck charm in the western world. Folklore tells that it brings good fortune to anyone who finds one, especially if they immediately give it to another person.

Florida Panthers™ coach Doug MacLean is a believer.

In April of 1996, MacLean's team was in New York, struggling to keep their playoff hopes alive, when the coach met an Irishman who gave him a four-leaf clover keychain. They not only beat the Rangers the next night, but went on to make the playoffs.

In his first season as coach of the Florida Panthers, MacLean took his team all the way to the Stanley Cup Finals beating the Bruins, Flyers and Penguins along the way. They lost in the finals, however, to Patrick Roy and the Colorado Avalanche™.

Maybe all those cats skating back and forth in front of the bench every night proved too much mojo for MacLean's lucky keychain.

TURK

Turk Wendell is tired of hearing the whispers, the comparisons floating down from the cheap seats like a gauzy wind during a slow-moving game. Turk, the whispers say, is really just The Bird of the 1990s. He is just the modern-day version of Mark "The Bird" Fidrych. Nothing more and nothing less. But Turk begs to differ. And the facts back him up - sure he likes to get down and manicure the mound, gently moving around the dirt just like The Bird used to do.

But Turk has other talents, other Mojo tendencies that keep him busy out on the ballfield. One of the most alarming things, if you aren't expecting it, is to stare into his mouth during a game he is pitching. See, the Turk likes to gnaw on four sticks of black licorice while on the mound. Then, if he has survived the inning, he likes to sprint toward the dugout - always, always, always hopping over the foul lines - and brush his teeth.

After some detailed attention to his molars, he likes to pop another four pieces of licorice in his mouth and retake the mound. Of course, he has learned to distinguish between so-called good batches of licorice and so-called bad batches of licorice - the bad batches are the ones he is chewing on when he is throwing lousy.

Turk's Mojo solution?

He throws away the licorice for the day - and then starts his licorice habit all over again for his next start.

THE LUCKY LUMBER

the whammer

Mojo Stick

Out of all the Tools of the Trade, it's the ultimate. It's also the most personal. And when someone bestows it on another player, it's like handing over a member of your family. It is, in the end, a sawed-off totem pole - bursting with meaning, symbolism and Mojo.

Hammerin' Hank Aaron - of whom it was said: it was harder to sneak a fastball by him than it was to sneak the sun by a rooster - used to take his bats from the Hillerich & Bradsby Company and cover them with sawdust. Then, the immortal home run king would secret his bats away in the attic, thinking that somehow, some way, this would make them more potent. Pete Rose, Mr. Charlie Hustle, had another bat ritual - he marinated as many as 24 bats at a time in motor oil, letting them soak for up to 30 days. He let them drip-dry and then put them in play, convinced that somehow they were also going to be harder, more resilient, more like Charlie Hustle himself. Sometimes, in what surely struck observers as a scary bit of Mojo, he could be spotted in the clubhouse rubbing a bone he was given by a butcher from New Jersey - Rose said he was doing it to tighten the grain on his bats, but it looked awfully symbolic.

In what might have been the ultimate statement about the Lucky Lumber, the great Orlando Cepeda considered each bat so special, each hit so special, that he had to discard his stick each time he stroked safely. The Mojo in each bat would be used up, Cepeda believed, each time another hit was squeezed out of it.

IF YOU JAR IT, HE WILL WIN

Long-time coach and pitcher Roger Craig wasn't alone. Like millions of movie fans, he thought that the flick "Field Of Dreams" was one of the better baseball movies ever made. The movie obviously had a lot to do with magic - something that Craig knew a bit about from his days with teams like the New York Mets™, the masters of outrageous wins and equally outrageous defeats.

Then, for a while, when Craig was managing the San Francisco Giants™, he had an especially unusual connection to the movie: Visitors to his office in Candlestick Park would notice a little jar on his desk. It had been sent to him by an anonymous fan and it was filled with dirt. Not ordinary dirt. It was Mojo Mud . . . it was dirt scooped from the very corn field in Iowa where they had filmed the movie "Field of Dreams."

Craig, not normally a superstitious type, decided the dirt had to stay when his Giants' launched into a nine-game winning streak. Craig even took the jar, on occasion, on road trips - though that Mighty Mojo Mud proved futile the day Terry Mulholland threw a no-hitter against Craig's team.

GOOD VIBRATIONS ON PICABO STREET

"I just wanna feel the vibe of the slope" - is how Picabo Street describes it when she skis slowly down a run that she will later be racing on. Picabo likes to survey the terrain just to gauge what "Vibe" a course will throw her way. One time, following knee surgery, Picabo was unable to ski hersel. So she hopped on her coach's back and let her coach do the skiing while she did the Vibe-checking.

Vibes and good Vibrations have always played a big deal in Street's family, ever since she got her colorful name from her ski-bum-hippie parents. As a child, her father once told Jean-Claude Killy: "I've got a daughter who's going to win a gold medal some day." Killy, the French god of skiing, sincerely replied: "Good for her, I hope she does."

At the 1998 Winter Olympics in Nagano, Japan, Picabo Street's deep belief in the Vibes was completely, utterly, reinforced when she was impatiently standing for her turn to walk up onto the awards-dais to accept her gold medal for winning the Super G. She felt the Vibes pass through her body when she saw it was Jean-Claude-Killy - the man her father had made a promise to when she was a little girl - who would be slipping the medal around her neck. "We Vibrate on a high level in our family." says Picabo.

BATH TIME

To suggest that Angelica Gavaldon has a superstitious nature
would be like saying 'Yogi the Bear' sort of likes picnic baskets.
Like most athletes, Angelica has always had her pre-match rituals. After winning a match she might eat the same
food, at the same restaurant, at the same table, with the same friend, until she was eliminated, or won the
tournament. Pretty pedestrian stuff. But as she started winning more, and the competition stiffened, the
pressure mounted, and the rituals became more frequent and a lot more bizarre.
When at home in Coronado, California, training between tournaments, Angelica would finish her
workout by driving around the tennis court parking lot exactly ten times before allowing herself to head for home.
While at Wimbledon in 1990, Gavaldon was staying with one of her mother's friends. Once every night, and once
every morning Angelica would have the friend kneel in the bathtub with her. "We weren't praying or anything
like that," she explained, "I just started overloading with weird, quirky stuff I felt I had to do,
or I'd lose my next match. It got so bad that I finally went to see a psychiatrist."
She didn't go the therapy route, but managed to rid herself of the superstitions on her own.
After taking a two-year break from the tour, Angelica is back in training.
Better get the tub ready, just in case.

The debate still rages about the sometimes unfine line that professional franchises (and plenty of so-called amateur programs at the collegiate level) dance between marketability and stereotypes: Debates crop up every year about whether the Washington Redskins™, the Cleveland Indians™ or the Atlanta Braves™ should change their names - after all, St. John's University decided that its teams should be called the Red Storm instead of the Redmen.

Whether zillionaire mogul Ted Turner was thinking about political correctness is hard to determine but back in 1982, he decided he had enough of one of the more identifiable (and controversial) mascots in all of sports. Turner wanted to ditch Chief Noc-A-Homa, the head-dressed and mocassined mascot who lived in a teepee out near the scoreboard.

Every time a Brave player would hit a homer the Chief would pop out of his teepee and do some sort of a dance. He was, obviously, kept very busy during the tenure of Hank Aaron.

According to some Atlanta news reports, Turner decided he didn't want the teepee and the Chief because he was looking to fill a few more seats in Atlanta-Fulton County Stadium. That August, when he ordered the teepee taken down, the Braves lost 19 of the following 21 games.

The teepee was restored. The Braves went on to win the Western Division.

Jerry Glanville is one of those coaches who has never been afraid to strike a different path.

Alternatively combative and charming, you never knew what you were going to get with Granville - but there was one

TICKETS for ELVIS

thing that was certain: If you were The King, you were going to

get two tickets to the big game.

For reasons that he never made entirely clear, Glanville used to

leave two tickets at the will-call window at the Houston

Astrodome for Elvis Presley. A handful of pretenders to the

throne would attempt to cash in on the tickets-in-waiting - but

without that special Elvis Presley driver's license, it was hard to

get in. A precise and indepth study of the correlation between

Elvis and the Houston Oilers'™ record under Glanville

has yet to be conducted. One thing is clear:

Elvis appeared to pick up his tickets about as often

as the Oilers' won the Super Bowl.

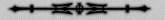

H ockey fans born pre-Watergate era probably remember exactly where they were the moment Mike Eruzione, captain of the 1980 U.S. Olympic hockey team, rifled a 30-foot wrist shot that beat Russian goalie Vladimir Myshkin and the seemingly invincible Soviet Union in a 4-3 victory that stunned the world. It was a win so inconceivable it has been known as the "Miracle On Ice" ever since.

Eruzione's inspired squad went on to beat Finland and net the second gold medal in U.S. Olympic hockey history.

But what if they hadn't won? What if Mike never made it out of the locker room for that game? Absurd you say? Maybe not.

The tenacious forward from Winthrop, Massachusetts had a number of pre-game rituals, including one superstition that theoretically could have kept him off the ice that historic day in 1980.

In addition to taping a lucky penny to the inside of his glove, Mike also liked to be the last player on the ice before a game, which was usually the case considering his main superstition. "I would chew a stick of gum and peel the foil from the wrapper in one perfect piece," Eruzione explains, "then I'd tie the foil to my skate and tape over it to secure the charm. If I tore the foil, I would start over with a fresh piece of gum, until I had a perfect sheet of foil. Sometimes it took a while, and a lot of gum, before I had it right."

Fortunately, for hockey fans throughout the United States, Mike's chewy-mojo ended his senior year at Boston University when the company that made the gum, changed the foil lining, making it impossible to peel.

The rest, as they say, is history.

ROLL *Out The* BARRELS

Suds and sports seem to go hand in hand. It's marketing that has been hand-crafted from the first days of professional athletics in America. But the legendary John McGraw, who coached the old New York Giants™, saw something deeper in the suds. Something more profound, intrinsic, mystical and Mojo Foamy. He saw the power of the beer barrel.

During a heated pennant race one of his sluggers, Mike Donlin, happened to spot a team of horses dutifully pulling along a truck that was crammed with empty beer barrels. The same day that Donlin spotted the beer barrel-toting horses outside of the long gone but not forgotten Polo Grounds, he collected four hits. He mentioned the coincidence to McGraw, one of the truly great students of seeking out the lucky edge in baseball. McGraw instantly knew what to do:

For the next straight 10 days, McGraw ordered wagons with empty beer barrels to pass by the New York stadium. And, in each game, Donlin continued to spray hits. McGraw told reporters that he had spent a small fortune to have the fake parade of beer-barrels. He also reminded them that his New York Giants scooped up the pennant.

ACME BREWERY
1888

INVOICE
245

n McGraw
ork Giants Baseball Club
Grounds

10 Round-Trip Transports To Ballpark By Wagon
With Load Of Empty Barrels.

Total $78.00

Back in the early 1990's,
The Wilkinson Sword Company conducted a locker room survey among NFL teams
to get a bead on player's pre-game rituals and grooming habits. Predictably, 'not shaving'
was one of the most common superstitions throughout most locker rooms.
The 'Whisker Mojo" however was far from exclusive to football. Athletes in many sports
believe that sparing the blade before competition gives an added edge.
Bjorn Borg's refusal to shave during a tournament until he was either eliminated,
or won it all, which was more often the case, was highly publicized and established
a 'fashion look' long before Don Johnson and Miami Vice came along. St. Louis Cardinals'™
hurler Al Hrabosky refused to cut his hair or beard during the entire season, earning him
the affectionate nickname 'Mad Hungarian'.
Most athletes willing to let their mojo down share a similar explanation:
Competition at the pro level is intense and calls for intense preparation. And whiskers
add that extra edge of intensity when putting on the 'game face'..

THE SAMSON EFFECT

PyRamid PoweR

For a while, Pyramid Power was the rage. Pyramids were supposed to ooze magical powers, healing powers, ancient powers. The truly faithful would even make the arduous trek up into the interior of the Egyptian pyramids so they could soak up the power right from the big-time source. And, even though it's hard to imagine now, somewhere in the pre-Viagra Era some folks believed that a carefully placed pyramid under the bed would restore a man's potency. Somehow, the pyramid had to find its way from the bedroom to the locker room:

When Red Kelly was coaching the Toronto Maple Leafs™, he was always on the hunt for something to give his skaters a Mojo Difference. In the mid-1970s, he thought he had finally found the ultimate key. It was Pyramid Power. For the '76 playoffs, he had team employees hang a huge pyramid from the ceiling inside the Toronto locker room. He also ordered something that he thought would give a complete pyramid power workout: he had smaller pyramids installed underneath the Toronto team bench. Kelly liked to think that the players could tap the pyramids while waiting to enter a game - and, literally, tap into some higher powers.

The saga of the Pyramid Power had a lucky ride and then an unfortunate end. The players and the coaches liked the pyramids right into the playoffs - but when the Philadelphia Flyers™ beat the Maple Leafs, the pyramids were trashed.

DAWG DAY AFTERNOON

Jerry Glanville has been one of the most durable coaches in professional sports - and he has built up a loyal legion of followers who swear by his every move on and off the field. Some of them, though, may be drawing the line at some Mojo Culinary events that have swirled around Glanville. They are moments that, shall we say, are in less-than-good-taste. They are also proof of the fact that what goes around comes around - and it might just sneak up behind you, when you least expect it, and take a big bite out your ego. Or, at least, a big bite of, well . . . . here's how the story goes:

One year when he was at the helm of the Houston Oilers™, head coach Glanville was chalking up X's and O's for an important contest against the Cleveland Browns™. While a gaggle of reporters stared in disbelief, Glanville suddenly decided to take a big bite on a dog biscuit - it was his way of saying he was going to take a big, heaping chunk out of the so-called Cleveland Browns' "Dawg Pound" - that hallowed group of Brownie fans who were among the most zealous in all of professional sports. This was, obviously, a pretty dicey, dangerous move on Glanville's part.

And, of course, the picture of him chewing on the dog biscuit was dutifully recorded by camera and sent around the country. Cleveland fans were stunned They collectively swore vengeance. Some of them went a little too far. Glanville's life was threatened. A security guard had to be posted outside of Glanville's room at the hotel where the Oilers were staying in Cleveland. He even wore a bulletproof vest when he entered the stadium. Right from the beginning, as soon as he appeared on the field, Glanville started getting some bad vibes - and worse. Fans hit him with snowballs - and dog biscuits - even before kickoff. Then, just minutes before the game was set to start, Glanville's Chewy Mojo came back to haunt him big time.

He didn't spot wide receiver Leonard Harris sprinting right toward him at full-speed during a warm-up. Harris ran his pass pattern straight into Glanville and sent the coach to the ground. Glanville blew out his knee. He had to coach the game in agonizing pain - and then he had to have surgery on the knee the next week.

"Big Dawg" John Thompson: "Hey...you come into another dog's yard with an attitude...you're gonna get bit!"

- RUBS THEM IN THE DIRT -

- YANKS HIS CAP -

The Road to Victory

Team owners, like their athletes and coaches, have been known to serve a mojo-master from time to time. And for many, what time they arrive at the stadium, and how they get to the stadium, can be just as important as getting there at all.

The late Chicago Cubs™ patriarch, P. K. Wrigley for instance, inadvertently took a very circuitous route home from the ballpark the night before his Cubs were to play an important double-header. The next day the Cubbies won both games and Wrigley faithfully drove home by that same route from then on.

Former Detroit Tigers™ owner Frank J. Navin, who once said, "Night baseball will be the beginning of the end for the major leagues", was being driven to Tiger Stadium one day when a black cat crossed in front of his car. Navin immediately ordered the driver to turn around and take him back home. When they arrived, Navin jumped out of the car, ran into his house, turned around, returned to the car and had the driver take him back the the ballpark by a completely different route.

Lucky Strikes

Joe Niekro was one-half of one of the greatest baseball-brother-combinations in the history of the game. Joe and brother Phil were known for being two of the most hard-nosed, fierce competitors on the mound – both of whom possessed arsenals which included a capricious, seductive and completely elusive, wicked knuckleball.

Little did anyone know that Joe had another weapon up his sleeve. Or in his carton. Maybe his pack. It turns out that Joe Niekro was throwing more than a ball that would look like it had suddenly fallen off the side of a table. Joe was throwing Lucky Strikes:

He liked to line up nine cigarettes, one by one, in the dugout and smoke one after he had knuckled his way through each inning. Joe set aside the nine, assuming of course he wasn't going to be pitching extra innings. Then, after he was off the mound and back in the dugout, he would fire up one of those smokes that were lined up like good soldiers.

"Nobody has ever given me a good, definite explanation as to why the ball does what it does," Niekro says. "Nobody's made me understand it."

Could be those Lucky Strikes.

HITTING THE CYCLE

Mojo can be, for some athletes, a cathartic undertaking. A way to rinse away blemishes on the soul - those imperfections that tend to roadblock your way to nirvana, or, at least hitting the cycle or racking up 200 yards rushing. Dave Concepcion, the legendary Cincinatti Reds™ shortstop, took it all to another dimension, another Mojo Plane, a completely dizzying and uncharted level.

Seems that Concepcion was sinking deeper into a funk about an inescapable hellhound of a batting slump. Nothing was working, including all those millions of bits of tinkering and micro-management by everyone watching him during batting practice. Concepcion was bankrupt in the hit department and the very fact was driving him to distraction.

Finally, as a joke, Concepcion crawled into a big industrial dryer - the kind the equipment managers use to dry a dozen sweaty jocks and uniforms. The ancient dryer suddenly started swirling - Pat Zachary was standing nearby and he had impishly tapped the *ON* button.

The upshot: The hair on Concepcion's arms was burned off - and so was his unlucky streak. Little Davey went on to hit like a madman after his cathartic experience in the spinning dryer.

THE HAKA

It is a war chant designed to instill fear in their opponents. It is a fervent prayer asking that they be protected. It is a pledge of honor to give total body and soul in the pursuit of victory. And as pre-game rituals go...the "HAKA" has no equal.

The HAKA, performed by both the New Zealand All Blacks and the Manu Samoan rugby teams in the photo above, is an ancient form of dance created by the Maori people of the South Pacific and held as a sacred form of art. It is a disciplined, emotional expression of the passion, vigour and identity of the Maori culture.

Though there are many styles of HAKA, the All Blacks rendition is for the most part Ka Mate, a short free-from style with some choreography characteristic of a traditional war dance. They have, however, taken a bit of license in order to make it more impressive and more appropriate to the game of rugby.

The HAKA was first performed by the All Blacks 'original' team in 1905 on their first overseas tour. It was also on this tour that the name 'All Blacks' was used. The HAKA became a permanent fixture for the All Blacks from then on.

The following is the HAKA performed by the Manu Samoan team (with a rough translation):

Manu!
Le Manu Samoa e, ia manu le fai o le faiva
Le Manu Samoa e, ia manu le fai o le faiva
Le Manu Samoa lenei ua ou sau
Leai se isi Manu o le atulaulau
Ua ou sau nei ma le mea atoa
Ma lo'u malosi ua atoatoa
Ia e faatisfa ma e soso ese
Leaga o lenei Manu e uiga ese
Le Manu Samoa! Le Manu Samoa!
Le Manu Samoa e o mai i Samoa!
Hi!

Hi! Warrior!
Samoan Warriors, may your endeavors be victorious.
Samoan Warriors, may your endeavors be victorious.
I am the Samoan Warrior I have arrived.
There is no other Warrior in the whole wide world.
I have come fully prepared (with the whole package),
And my strength is supreme.
You must make way and move aside,
Because this Warrior is extraordinary.
The Samoan Warrior! The Samoan Warrior!
The Samoan Warriors are from Samoa!
He!

THE STOMP

The 'Stomp' is a tradition that is so completely British, it plays out like a scene from a Monty Python film.

It has been performed every morning of a 'Bumps' (competition) day by members of the Lady Margaret Boat Club

of St. John's College (University of Cambridge), since the beginning of rowing as a sport.

The ritual begins when all the crews scheduled to compete that day line up dressed in the formal boat club tenure - bright red blazers

with brass buttons - and march up to the 'Stomp' or 'Bumps' tree in the gardens of St. John's.

With fists clenched, the rowers then hit the tree three times while shouting the name of the crew they have to bump that day.

Once the tree has been properly 'stomped', the crew then marches through the grounds of their main rival, Trinity College.

The crews from Trinity perform a similar ritual at the same time, which ultimately takes them into the grounds of

St. John's, where, somewhere along the way, the rival crews meet and engage in a good-natured brawl.

They shove and tackle each other for a minute or so, then pick themselves up and head off to breakfast.

"The overall atmosphere of the 'Stomp' is one of good fun", explains St. John's oarsman Nick Geddes,

"There are rarely any injuries. It is an acknowledgement of the age-old rivalry between Trinity and St. John's."

"The one time the 'Stomp' was not carried out," former crew captain Carsten Zatschler recalls,

"four of our club's boats were 'bumped', while the other three sank." Bad show!

Lets face it, athletes demand a lot from their bodies.

Forget about the broken bones, bruised muscles and torn ligaments that can afflict even those in the best of condition. We're talking about the basic stresses that occur in the course of a routine workout. Athletes drain their natural sodium reserves through excessive sweating, causing rapid and potentially dangerous dehydration.

Most athletes try to counter these effects by drinking those brightly colored, scientifically formulated sports drinks, the beverages designed to rehydrate the body with electrolytes and carbohydrates, and help the body maintain the balance needed for optimum physiological function.

An Indonesian runner named Ruwiyati, however, prefers to refresh herself with something a little more basic and a lot more bizarre.

After winning the marathon in the Southeast Asian Games in 1997, Ruwiyati promptly informed reporters that the secret to her success is that she drinks blood from her coach Alwi Mugiyanto's finger before each race. "I don't know why, but she just insists on doing it," a bemused Mugiyanto explained.

NFL coaches beware, if Ruwiyati's blood ritual becomes *de rigueur* with football players, the next Gatorade-dump could be a *real* "blood bath."

The Pause that Refreshes

Mojo Hall of Fame...

IN THE ROSTER OF MOJO MEN, IT'S HARD TO IMAGINE ANY SINGLE INDIVIDUAL STANDING TALLER THAN MARK "THE BIRD" FIDRYCH. THOUGH TODAY HE TENDS TO NOT DWELL ON HIS LOQUACIOUS PAST, FIDRYCH ENCHANTED THE SPORTS WORLD IN THE MID-1970S WHEN HE WOUND UP WITH A NICE FASTBALL AND A TRICK BAG OF MOJO MANNERISMS FOR THE DETROIT TIGERS™

WHEN HE EXPLODED ON THE SCENE IN 1976, THE BIRD WAS INSTANTLY KNOWN FOR MORE THAN JUST BEING ABLE TO GET PEOPLE OUT FAIRLY REGULARLY (HE STARTED THE ALL-STAR GAME™ AS A ROOKIE AND WENT ON TO WIN 19 GAMES AND A.L. ROOKIE OF THE YEAR HONORS). PEOPLE LINED UP EARLY AT BALLPARKS AROUND THE COUNTRY JUST TO MAKE SURE THEY COULD GET A TICKET TO SEE THE BIRD TALK TO THE BALL, HAND-SCULPT THE DIRT ON THE MOUND AND GO THROUGH A RANGE OF MOJO MANNERISMS THAT HAD OLD-TIMERS ROLLING THEIR EYES FROM OPPOSING DUGOUTS.

NO ONE IN BASEBALL IN THE LAST THREE DECADES WAS SO PERFECTLY WILLING TO LAY HIS MOJO OUT SO PUBLICLY. BIRD WASN'T SHY ABOUT HIS ONE-SIDED CONVERSATIONS WITH THE BALL HE WAS ABOUT TO PITCH. WITH THOUSANDS OF PEOPLE WATCHING, HE LAID IT ALL OUT IN THE OPEN. WHILE HE CHATTED WITH THE BALL, THE WORLD SEEMED TO JUST STAND STILL.

MARK FIDRYCH WAS OUT OF THE GAME BY THE AGE OF 25, BUT NOBODY CAN DENY THE FACT THAT THE SUMMER OF '76 BELONGED TO THE BIRD.

Stock Car racing has its share of Mojo Moments - Joe Weatherly liked to be paid his share of purses in silver dollars, Glenn "Fireball" Roberts refused to have his wife kiss him before a race. A slew of drivers stayed away from peanuts and the color green. But nothing compares to the fateful day of 'The Voice'.

Talladega, Alabama is one of the most important sporting stops in the nation - it is home to one of the premier races in the extraordinarily popular, ever-growing world of motor sports. It is also where one of the most unusual bits of Racing Mojo went down - and it all happened to involve the immortal Bobby Isaac, one of the greatest drivers to ever strap himself inside the fastest cars known to man.

Isaac, known as one of the most nervy competitors on the stock-car track, was racing in the Winston 500 in 1973 at Talladega. The race was going well, nothing out of the ordinary - except, of course, for the rocketing speeds. Suddenly, inside his helmet, Isaac heard a voice. It wasn't his pit crew telling him to slow down, re-fuel or change a tire. There wasn't anything wrong with his car. But, Isaac heard the voice: "Park Your Car."

So, mid-way through the 500 lap race, Isaac obeyed the voice.

He pulled the car into the garage area. The future Hall of Famer (he was inducted into the International Motorsports Hall of Fame in 1996) got out of his car and never ran in a Winston Cup race again.

THE VOICE

EL TIANTE

| 2,416 STRIKE OUTS | 3.30 LIFETIME E.R.A. | | 229-172 RECORD | 4-TIME 20 GAME WINNER |

Luis Tiant was probably known more for his charismatic style than for his legacy as one of the greatest pitchers in the history of the game. "El Tiante", as he was affectionately known to his legions of adoring Red Sox™ fans, possessed a blazing fastball and a trademark 'corkscrew' delivery that had him facing second base more often than home plate.

While it was his ability to mow down batters in quick order that made him great, it was his intimidating fu manchu mustache, post-game cigars in the shower, and penchant for reaching into his locker full of mojo that most us will remember. Among his many superstitions, Luis wore strands of beads and a special loin cloth around the waist under his uniform, to 'ward off evil'. Though he played for a total of six different teams throughout his career, his best season was with the Cleveland Indians™ in 1968, when he posted a 21-9 record with a 1.60 earned run average.

While Tiant may wind up being the best pitcher never to make it into the Baseball Hall of Fame in Cooperstown, we are proud to induct "El Tiante" into the Hall of Fame of Locker Room Mojo.

A bell tower on a dark, stormy night. Rain blown sideways by winds howling unearthly tones. Suddenly, in a flash of lightning we see a disfigured silhouette of a man atop the tower, moving uneasily towards the edge.

CUT:

Ok, that's the image Hollywood has planted in our collective psyche. The image that rockets forth at the mere mention of the word 'hunchback'.

Sadly, in the early days of baseball, hunchbacks, like cross-eyed people, were considered very unlucky. Just to lay eyes on one meant bad mojo for the viewer.

While the origin of this prejudice remains unclear, perhaps the luckiest mascot in baseball history was a boy with a badly malformed spine by the name of Eddie Bennett.

Eddie joined the infamous Chicago White Sox™ in 1919, serving as their official bat boy. He traveled with the team, tending their bats, and making himself generally useful. The Sox won the pennant with Eddie aboard, but as history well remembers, they tanked the World Series™ to the Cincinnati Reds™.

The next season Eddie signed on with the Brooklyn Dodgers™, apparently taking his lucky ways with him, the Dodgers won the National League™ pennant. Unfortunately, for reasons that go unexplained, during the World Series they left Eddie in Brooklyn when they embarked for Cleveland with 2-1 lead in games. The Indians won four straight and the championship.

Bennett jumped ship and hooked up with the New York Yankees™ the following year, changing teams for the third straight season.

It is said that Babe Ruth, never one to overlook a gift from lady luck, liked to rub Eddie's 'charmed hump' before going to the plate.

The Yankees won three consecutive pennants, giving Eddie the distinction of lugging lumber for five flag-winning clubs in five years, and making him the luckiest mascot baseball has ever seen.

EDDIE BENNETT

Fear of Flying

Jackie Jensen was a very good baseball player.

He was so good that from 1954 to 1959, the Boston Red Sox™ slugger had more runs batted in than anyone else in the American League™, including the great Mickey Mantle, and his own teammate Ted Williams.

Major League Baseball™ thought he was so good, they named him the American League's Most Valuable Player in 1958.

But in 1961 Jensen up and quit the game at the age of 32. He wasn't injured. He wasn't burned out on baseball. Jackie was simply afraid of flying.

When he started playing professional baseball, teams still traveled by train. Eventually, as the clubs switched to airplane travel, Jackie was forced to either cope with flying or find other ways to get from city to city. He once drove over 800 miles from Boston to Detroit to avoid flying. Desperate, Jensen retained a psychiatrist, and even tried hypnosis to conquer his fear.

But nothing worked.

Jackie Jensen left baseball with 1463 hits, 929 RBI's and a slugging average of .460, his career grounded early by the fear of flying.

Smith Gets Assist In Flyer's Success

In arenas and stadiums across the United States the 'Great American Debate' continues over nachos and frothy beer...whether to replace the 'Star Spangled Banner', our current national anthem, with Irving Berlin's 'God Bless America'. Both equally patriotic, the question remains: which tune best exemplifies the United States of America?

While the debate will probably never be settled on a national scale, the Philadelphia Flyers™ have bucked tradition and gone their own way. It began on December 11, 1969 when they played a tape of Kate Smith's rendition of Berlin's masterpiece before a game. Nobody sang it better than Smith. Its a classic. To record anyone else singing it would be a sacrilege to say the least. And in mojo terms... it has paid off big time.

The Flyers have enjoyed incredible success in games when Kate Smith sang, especially in 1974 and 75 when they won the Stanley Cup™ back to back.

Even long after Smith passed away, she brought Dame fortune to the Spectrum. Before games 3 and 6 of the 1987 Stanley Cup finals against Edmonton, Smith's voice rattled the Spectrum rafters and they won in come-from-behind fashion in both games.

the human rain delay

Time.   Some athletes can stretch it, play with it, mend it and bend it. The best ones, of course, make time stand still - or, to be correct, they tend to suspend everyone else around them in some sort of state of interrupted animation. Then, while everyone else is frozen, the truly greats --- from Muhammad Ali to Michael Jordan - go to work. The truly greats own time. And, plenty of athletes spend inordinate amounts of time, well, trying to control time:

Mike Hargrove, when he played with the Cleveland Indians™ and the Texas Rangers™, was nicknamed the "human rain delay" because he spent so much time on his rituals, superstitions and Mojo Moments. Hargrove liked to start off by strolling up and down the first base line, taking exactly three practice swings. He would follow up by digging a hole in the batter's box with his left foot. He would take the sweat off his lip with his left elbow. He would adjust his left batting glove. He would tug on his right shoulder and hitch up his pants with his left hand. The best part of all - if the pitcher still wasn't ready, then Hargrove would go through the ritual one more time.

PICTURE CREDITS

About the Authors

Nick Newton, a native of Chicago, Illinois,
has worked for over twenty years in the entertainment industry
creating marketing campaigns and title sequences
for film and television.
A freelance graphic designer, he now lives in Austin, Texas
with his wife and two daughters.

Bill Minutaglio is a veteran journalist, author and contributing writer
to The Sporting News. His work has been cited in the books:
"The Best of American Sports Writing 1997"
and "The Best of American Sports Writing 1998."
In addition to having been a senior writer and columnist for The Dallas Morning News,
Bill's work has appeared in many publications including The Los Angeles Times,
DETAILS, and The Bulletin of The Atomic Scientist.

To order this book
directly from the publisher,
visit our website @
www.lockerroommojo.com

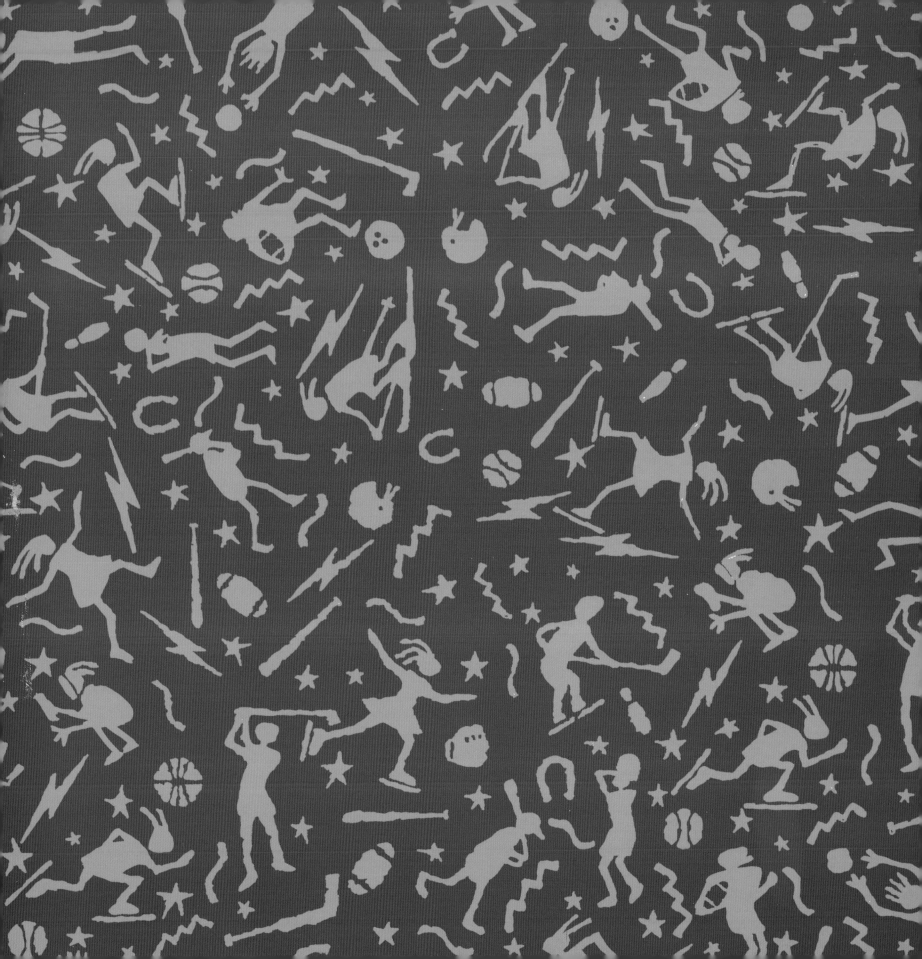

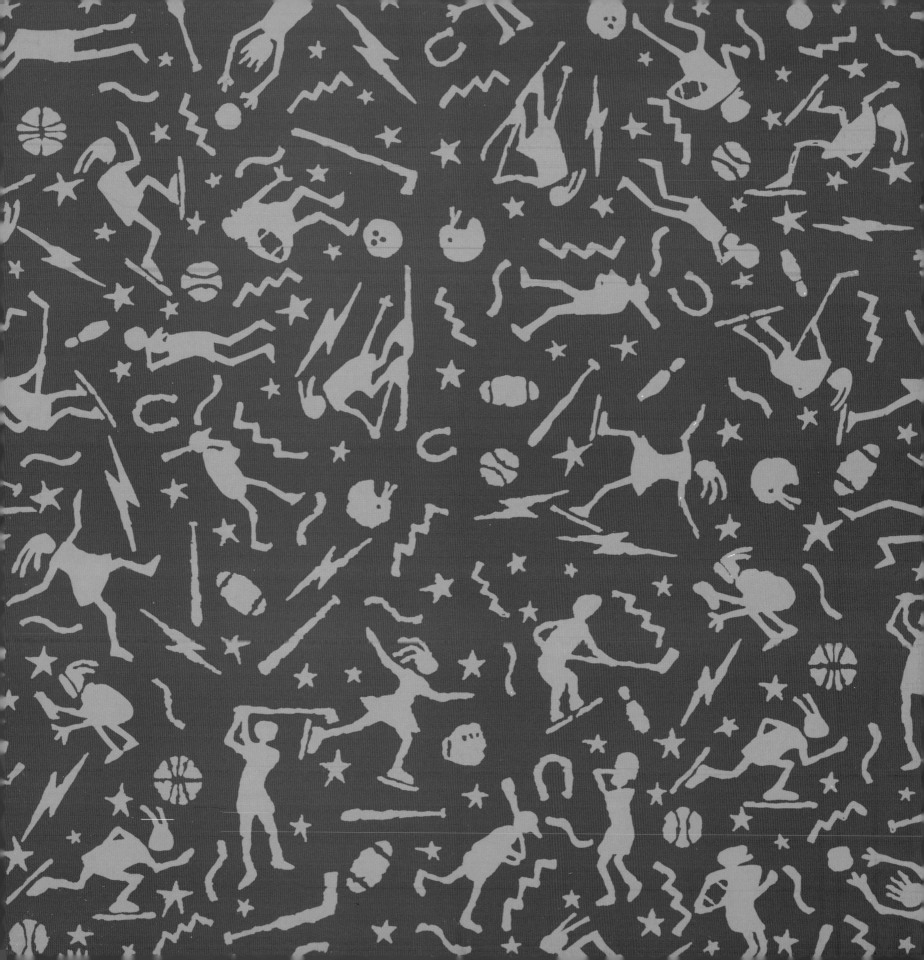